W9-CDX-523

**Cultural And
Geographical
Exploration**

Touring America
Seventy-Five
Years Ago

CHRONICLES FROM *NATIONAL GEOGRAPHIC*

Cultural And Geographical Exploration

Cultural And Geographical Exploration

Touring America Seventy-Five Years Ago

How the Automobile and the Railroad Changed the Nation

CHRONICLES FROM *NATIONAL GEOGRAPHIC*

Arthur M. Schlesinger, jr.
Senior Consulting Editor

Fred L. Israel
General Editor

CHELSEA HOUSE PUBLISHERS

Philadelphia

CHELSEA HOUSE PUBLISHERS

Editor in Chief Stephen Reginald
Managing Editor James D. Gallagher
Production Manager Pamela Loos
Art Director Sara Davis
Director of Photography Judy L. Hasday
Senior Production Editor Lisa Chippendale

First Printing

1 3 5 7 9 8 6 4 2

Library of Congress Cataloging-in-Publication Data

Touring America seventy-five years ago: how the automobile and the
railroad changed the nation: chronicles from National Geographic/
Arthur M. Schlesinger, jr., senior consulting editor. Fred L. Israel,
general editor.
    p.   cm.—(Cultural and geographical exploration)
Includes bibliographical references and index.
Summary: Articles originally published in "National Geographic" chart
the expansion of travel by automobile and railroad in the 1920s and
its effects on American society.
ISBN 0-7910-5098-X
1. Automobiles—Social aspects—United States—Juvenile literature.
2. Railroads—Social aspects—United States—Juvenile literature.
3. Americans—Travel—Juvenile literature.   [1. Automobiles—
History. 2. Railroads—History.]   I. Schlesinger, Arthur Meier, 1917– .
II. Israel, Fred L. III. National Geographic Society (U.S.) IV. Series.
HE5623.T58   1998
303.48'32—dc21   98-31793
                                                            CIP
                                                            AC

CONTENTS

"THE GREATEST EDUCATIONAL JOURNAL"

When the first *National Geographic* magazine appeared in October 1888, the United States totaled 38 states. Grover Cleveland was President. The nation's population hovered around 60 million. Great Britain's Queen Victoria also ruled as the Empress of India. William II became Kaiser of Germany that year. Tsar Alexander III ruled Russia and the Turkish Empire stretched from the Balkans to the tip of Arabia. To Westerners, the Far East was still a remote and mysterious land. Throughout the world, riding the back of an animal was the principle means of transportation. Unexplored and unmarked places dotted the global map.

On January 13, 1888, thirty-three men—scientists, cartographers, inventors, scholars, and explorers—met in Washington, D. C. They had accepted an invitation from Gardiner Greene Hubbard (1822-1897), the first president of the Bell Telephone Co. and a leader in the education of the deaf, to form the National Geographic Society "to increase and diffuse geographic knowledge." One of the assembled group noted that they were the "first explorers of the Grand Canyon and the Yellowstone, those who had carried the American flag farthest north, who had measured the altitude of our famous mountains, traced the windings of our coasts and rivers, determined the distribution of flora and fauna, enlightened us in the customs of the aborigines, and marked out the path of storm and flood." Nine months later, the first issue of *National Geographic* magazine was sent out to 165 charter members. Today, more than a century later, membership has grown to an astounding 11 million in more than 170 nations. Several times that number regularly read the monthly issues of the *National Geographic* magazine.

The first years were difficult ones for the new magazine. The earliest volumes seem dreadfully scientific and quite dull. The articles in Volume I, No. 1 set the tone—W. M Davis, "Geographic Methods in Geologic Investigation," followed by W. J. McGee, "The Classification of Geographic Forms by Genesis." Issues came out erratically—three in 1889, five in 1890, four in 1891; and two in 1895. In January 1896 "an illustrated monthly" was added to the title. The November issue that year contained a photograph of a half-naked Zulu bride and bridegroom in their wedding finery staring full face into the camera. But, a reader must have wondered what to make of the accompanying text: "These people . . . possess some excellent traits, but are horribly cruel when once they have smelled blood." In hopes of expanding circulation, the Board of Managers offered newsstand copies at $.25 each and began to accept advertising. But the magazine essentially remained unchanged. Circulation only rose slightly.

In January 1898, shortly after Gardiner Greene Hubbard's death, his son-in-law Alexander Graham Bell (1847-1922) agreed to succeed him as the second president of the National Geographic Society. Bell invented the telephone in 1876 and, while pursuing his life long goal of improving the lot of the deaf, had turned his amazingly versatile mind to contemplating such varied problems as human flight, air conditioning, and popularizing geography. The society then had about 1100 members—the magazine was on the edge of bankruptcy. Bell did not want the job. He wrote in his diary though that he accepted leadership of the Society "in order to save it. Geography is a fascinating subject and it can be made interesting," he told the board of directors. Bell abandoned the unsuccessful attempt to increase circulation through newsstand sales. "Our journal," he wrote "should go to members, people who believe in our work and want to help." He understood that the lure for prospective members should be an association with a society that made it possible for the average person to share with kings and scientists the excitement of sending an expedition to a strange land or an explorer to an inaccessible region. This idea, more than any other, has been responsible for the growth of the National Geographic Society and for the popularity of the magazine. "I can well remember," recalled Bell in 1912, "how the idea was laughed at that we should ever reach a membership of ten thousand." That year it had soared to 107,000!

Bell attributed this phenomenal growth though to one man who had transformed the *National Geographic* magazine into "the greatest educational journal in the world"—Gilbert H. Grosvenor (1875-1966). Bell had hired the then 24-year-old Grosvenor in 1899 as the Society's first full-time employee "to put some life into the magazine." He personally escorted the new editor, who will become his son-in-law, to the Society's headquarters—a small rented room shared with the American Forestry Association on the fifth floor of a building, long since gone, across 15th street from the U. S. Treasury in downtown Washington. Grosvenor remembered the headquarters "littered with old magazines, newspapers, and a few record books and six enormous boxes crammed with *Geographics* returned by the newsstands." "No desk!" exclaimed Bell. "I'll send you mine." That afternoon, delivery men brought Grosvenor a large walnut rolltop and the new editor began to implement Bell's instructions—to transform the magazine from one of cold geographic fact "expressed in hieroglyphic terms which the layman could not understand into a vehicle for carrying the living, breathing, human-interest truth about this great world of ours to the people." And what did Bell consider appropriate "geographic subjects?" He replied: "The world and all that is in it is our theme."

Grosvenor shared Bell's vision of a great society and magazine which would disseminate geographic knowledge. "I thought of geography in terms of its Greek root: *geographia*—a description of the world," he later wrote. "It thus becomes the most catholic of subjects, universal in appeal, and embracing nations, people, plants, birds, fish. We would never lack interesting subjects." To attract readers, Grosvenor had to change the public attitude toward geography which he knew was regarded as "one of the dullest of all subjects, something to inflict upon schoolboys and avoid in later life." He wondered why certain books which relied heavily on geographic description remained popular—Charles Darwin's *Voyage of the Beagle*, Richard Dana, Jr.'s *Two Years Before the Mast* and even Herodotus' *History*. Why did readers for generations, and with Herodotus' travels, for twenty centuries return to these books? What did these volumes, which used so many geographic descriptions, have in common? What was the secret? According to Grosvenor, the answer was that "each was an accurate, eyewitness, firsthand account. Each contained simple straightforward writing—writing that sought to make pictures in the reader's mind."

Gilbert Grosvenor was editor of the *National Geographic* magazine for 55 years, from 1899 until 1954. Each of the 660 issues under his direction had been a highly readable geography textbook. He took Bell's vision and made it a reality. Acclaimed as "Mr. Geography," he discovered the earth anew for himself and for millions around the globe. He charted the dynamic course which the National Geographic Society and its magazine followed for more than half a century. In so doing, he forged an instrument for world education and understanding unique in this or any age. Under his direction, the *National Geographic* magazine grew from a few hundred copies—he recalled carrying them to the post office on his back—to more than five million at the time of his retirement as editor, enough for a stack 25 miles high.

This Chelsea House series celebrates Grosvenor's first twenty-five years as editor of the *National Geographic*. "The mind must see before it can believe," said Grosvenor. From the earliest days, he filled the magazine with photographs and established another Geographic principle—to portray people in their natural attire or lack of it. Within his own editorial committee, young Grosvenor encountered the prejudice that photographs had to be "scientific." Too often, this meant dullness. To Grosvenor, every picture and sentence had to be interesting to the layman. "How could you educate and inform if you lost your audience by boring your readers?" Grosvenor would ask his staff. He persisted and succeeded in making the *National Geographic* magazine reflect this fascinating world.

To the young-in-heart of every age there is magic in the name *National Geographic*. The very words conjure up enchanting images of faraway places, explorers and scientists, sparkling seas and dazzling mountain peaks, strange plants, animals, people, and customs. The small society founded in 1888 "for the increase and diffusion of geographic knowledge" grew, under the guidance of one man, to become a great force for knowledge and understanding. This achievement lies in the genius of Gilbert H. Grosvenor, the architect and master builder of the National Geographic Society and its magazine.

Fred L. Israel
The City College of the City University of New York

TOURING AMERICA: AN OVERVIEW

Fred L. Israel

By 1920 the United States had achieved the highest standard of living any nation had ever known. National income soared from $480 per capita in 1900 to $681 in 1929. Workers were paid the highest wages of any time in the country's history. Between 1922 and 1927 the economy grew by seven percent a year, the largest peacetime growth rate ever. Industrial technology was partly responsible. All over the nation, old machines were being junked for new ones. Steam turbines and steam shovels, electric motors, belt conveyors, and countless other automatic and semiautomatic machinery replaced manual workers each year. Even so, the labor force grew at a faster rate than the population. In 1914, for example, Henry Ford installed the first moving assembly line with a chain conveyor. Within three months, his workers were assembling an automobile in 93 minutes. A year before it had taken 14 hours. By 1925, the process had been so well refined that a Model T automobile rolled off the Ford assembly line every 10 seconds. At $290, compared to $845 before total automation, almost anyone could afford one.

The automobile now competed with railroads for passengers. Soon single cars operated by gasoline motors began displacing local trains as new roads made it possible to settle beyond the traditional walking-accessible city. In 1919 Oregon, Mexico, and Colorado hit upon a new idea for financing road construction—a tax on gasoline. Within a decade, every state had one. In 1920, only 7,000 miles of hard-surface roads existed; seven years later, there were 50,000; and by 1928, a tourist could drive from New York to Kansas and never leave a paved highway. To recover their passengers, railroads began providing finer coaches and more comfortable sleepers. Then came the streamlined train with luxurious accommodations. Prosperity for many, the automobile, and the passenger train combined to make the 1920s a decade of travel and tourism for middle-class Americans.

The automobile and the railroad sped Americans to work, took them on their vacations, and lessened their isolation from one another. Railroad companies promoted pleasure excursions and millions now took trains to vacation spots. Trains romantically named the Twentieth Century Limited and the Seashore were advertised as the ultimate in passenger safety and comfort. Likewise, glossy magazine stories promoted automobile travel. For example, throughout the 1920s *National Geographic* frequently included articles on the Far West that undoubtedly contributed to Americans traveling longer distances for pleasure.

The United States government also assisted recreational travel and tourism through the creation of the national park system. The opening of Yellowstone Park in 1872 was soon followed by the creation of other national parks. By 1916 there were 16, with a total of 7,400 square miles. Thirteen years later, there were 25 national parks totaling more than 16,000 square miles. A new type of business, travel agencies, now arranged tours for individuals and groups.

At the beginning of the 20th century, only the most adventurous dared the perils of long distance automobile travel. With flimsy tires and undependable motors, as well as mud holes and few gas stations, breakdowns were frequent. Gradually, as conditions improved, the touring horizon widened. As automobile ownership grew, touring increased. However, transcontinental travel developed very slowly, largely due to inadequate roads. As late as 1928, a leading travel magazine urged motorists starting for the West Coast to carry a shovel, tow rope, fuel cans, and an adequate supply of food and water.

As the decade ended, though, automobile pleasure traveling had become a great national pastime. Better roads, ample accommodations, dependable vehicles, and a network of service stations brought about the phenomenon of millions of Americans moving back and forth in search of new scenes and surroundings.

In 1920 about 9 million automobiles were registered in the United States. Ten years later, it was nearly 30 million. Many Americans came to see the automobile as part of their minimum standard of living. For some, it became a status symbol. In Sinclair Lewis's *Main Street*, the hero admits to four loves: his wife, his medical practice, hunting, and his automobile. He could not rank them in order of preference.

Vol. XLIV, No. 4   WASHINGTON   October, 1923

THE AUTOMOBILE INDUSTRY

An American Art That Has Revolutionized Methods in Manufacturing and Transformed Transportation

By William Joseph Showalter

Author of "The Panama Canal," "How the World is Fed," "Industry's Greatest Asset—Steel," "Coal—Ally of American Industry," "America's Amazing Railway Traffic," etc., in the National Geographic Magazine

The following article presents a careful survey of the economic consequences of the development of the motor vehicle and a layman's impressions of the highly technical automobile manufacturing industry. The latter were gained during months of observation and inspection in the largest automobile factories in America, under the guidance of automotive engineers and manufacturing superintendents.—The Editor.

WITH thirteen million motor cars and trucks now running on the roads of the United States, and with the annual demand for new ones in excess of three millions, America is both literally and figuratively "stepping on the gas" in the making of transportation history.

A quarter of a century has brought a development in the automobile industry that has out-run the dreamers, confounded the prophets, and amazed the world.

In 1898 there was one car in operation for every eighteen thousand people, each of them a hybrid creation secured by crossing a bicycle with a buggy, and installing in the product a noisy, sputtering little engine that startled the people in the streets and sent the horses on the highways into panic.

A PICTURESQUE PIECE OF ROAD-BUILDING ON SIGNAL MOUNTAIN, TENNESSEE

To-day there is one motor vehicle to every eight people, and the worst of them is a marvel of silence and service as compared with the best of its early predecessors.

Thirteen million motor cars! Who can visualize them! Five for every freight and passenger car on all the railroads of the United States! Enough to carry half the people of America in a single caravan!

The Lincoln Highway, from the banks of the Hudson to the Golden Gate, is 3,305 miles long. To put them all on that highway, even in traffic-jam formation, would require that it be widened so that fifteen cars could stand abreast!

ROUND TRIP TO THE SUN
EVERY 21 HOURS

The service they render is proportionately large. Assuming that the average car is operated only ten months in a year and runs only twenty miles a day, their aggregate travel amounts to seventy-eight billion miles annually.

Such a mileage figure being so vast, we might conclude that ten months a year and twenty miles a day overestimated the average car's performance, but both gas and tire data tend to justify an even greater mileage.

It is estimated that the gas consumption by the motor cars of the country will exceed six billion gallons this year. It is generally held that, taking every type of car, the average driver is able to coax fifteen miles out of each gallon

A POWER MACHINE OF THE FIRST MAGNITUDE:
A PRESENT-DAY TYPE OF RACING CAR READY FOR THE BIG RUN

Many of the racing cars are one-man vehicles, with a cockpit into which the driver can crouch in the event of a mishap. In some cars a sector is eliminated from the steering wheel rim to enable the driver to get his body completely into the cockpit, in the event the car rolls over.

THE LINE-UP AT THE START OF THE SPEEDWAY 500-MILE TEST AT INDIANAPOLIS

"These terrific tests have always brought the engineering talent of the country together. Under the lessons learned there, cylinder displacement has been reduced, fuel economy has been evolved, and safety has been forged into every element of your car and mine, on the mighty anvil of a speedway and under the powerful hammer of high speed. Harmony, balance, dependability, tire mileage, and sturdiness have come from the flaming forge of a hundred miles an hour" (see text, page 45).

DOWN THE STRETCH WITH THROTTLES WIDE OPEN

No phase of motor-car development has brought more comfort to the car-owner than the evolution of tire dependability. In the big speedway races there is an amazing amount of skidding around the turns, and tires simply had to be improved to stand the grind. The long life that every motorist now finds in high-grade tires grew out of lessons learned in these grueling races.

THE START OF THE HARKNESS TROPHY RACE
AT THE SHEEPSHEAD BAY SPEEDWAY, NEW YORK

Where once the kings and queens of the turf thrilled the multitudes with the fleetness of horse flesh, now the finest creations of the automotive engineer's art flash around the course at a hundred miles an hour.

of gas he puts into his tank. But even on the basis of thirteen miles per gallon, a little arithmetic gives the enormous total mentioned above.

It is also believed that the average tire, fabrics and cords, delivers more than 8,000 miles of service. On the basis of the number of tires put on automotive wheels annually, the aggregate motor-car mileage would be eighty billions.

Three times as many motor-miles on the highways as car-miles on the railways is a marvelous record for so youthful a competitor of rail transportation.

Counts at the New York City ferries and elsewhere indicate that the average car carries 2½ passengers. This means that more than thirty million people take to automotive wheels every day, or more than nine billion annually—eight times as many as are carried by all the railroads.

The transformation in the lives of the people which these figures indicate stands almost, if not quite, unparalleled in any quarter of a century of human existence.

Starting out as a plaything, transformed into a luxury, and then becoming, in turn, a definite element in our standard of living, the motor vehicle has assumed the rôle of a highly efficient factor in our transportation system, touching the lives and promoting the welfare of America as few developments in the history of any nation have done.

TRANSPORTATION
THE LADDER OF CIVILIZATION

Transportation, some one has well said, has been the ladder upon which humanity climbed from a condition of primitive life to that of a finely wrought and complex civilization.

As the number of automobiles has grown, the wealth of the country has increased. In 1909 we had less than three hundred thousand motor vehicles in commission and the national income amounted to less than twenty-nine billion dollars. To-day, with our thirteen million registered vehicles, the national income is around sixty billion dollars.

AT THE END OF THE TRAIL: GLACIER POINT, YOSEMITE PARK, CALIFORNIA

Through the automobile, the American people have broken the bonds that formerly tied them to narrow localities.

BESIDE A MOUNTAIN OF ICE
CAST UPON THE SHORE OF GREEN BAY, NEAR ESCANABA, MICHIGAN

Ninety per cent of the public buy their cars from 20 per cent of the manufacturers. The other 80 per cent of the manufacturers divide the remaining 10 per cent of the sales among them. But catering to the 10 per cent who want something different means a trade worth more than half a billion dollars a year.

CAUGHT IN A SNOWSTORM ON THE RIM OF CRATER LAKE, OREGON

The cost of parts replacements in motor cars of the present day is surprisingly low, in spite of the high cost of installation. One major manufacturer shows that all parts sales for the year amounted to only $13 per car. This is wholesale, of course.

Although we are, as a nation, according to Moody, the statistician, spending more for our automobile service than is being spent for railroad transportation, shelter, or heat and light—more, indeed, than for any other item in our national budget except clothing and meats—our savings-bank deposits and every other index of economic well-being tell the same story of the growth of our national wealth.

Economic readjustments are taking place on a major scale, and with increasing momentum, under the irresistible impact of automotive mileage.

Cities are spreading out. Long Island is built up for half its length to accommodate those who make New York the metropolis of America; so is New Jersey from Morristown to Long Branch and from Jersey City to the Empire State boundary at Suffern. Even Connecticut, as far as Stamford, Greenwich, and New Canaan, is peopled with those who work in Gotham by day and sleep in the country by night.

A ROPE-TIRED HYDROCARBON CARRIAGE OF THE 1899 TYPE

When Charles Goodyear accidentally dropped a lump of his rubber compound on a hot stove, he little dreamed of the forty million cord and fabric tires that would annually rise out of his discovery, or of the motor-car industry made possible thereby.

**A CROSS BETWEEN A BICYCLE AND A BUGGY,
IN THE EARLY DAYS OF THE AUTOMOTIVE INDUSTRY**

Haynes, Ford, Duryea, Winton, Olds, and Apperson are names that will live as the founders of a vast industry who builded better than they knew.

Chicago has the same story to tell, with its scores of consequential colonies, its dozens of outlying subdivisions. Philadelphia and San Francisco are but other examples of how men are coming to work in town and live in the country.

Not only in a residential way are cities undergoing a change, but also in a business way. The trek of branch banks far out beyond the business district is but one straw showing the direction of the transportation wind. The lack of parking space down town is making an ever-widening business district and new centers of commercial activity in every major urban community. The era of down-town crowding is forcing the future to change radically our orthodox type of commercial concentration.

EVER-BROADENING RURAL HORIZONS

A similar transition is occurring on the farm. No longer are the farmer's children isolated. They can find their diversion in the pleasures of urban life after the day's rural tasks are done.

High schools are spreading out through the rural districts, and the general substitution of systematic secondary education for the little red schoolhouse type of training is of vast moment to America.

EXPERIMENTAL TRANSPORTATION TWO DECADES AGO

The blacksmith and the owner of a one-hoss shay survey with disdain the new-fangled machine which presumes to travel rubber-shod over rough highways. And for many seasons, before the day of perfected motor and of service station, it was the horse or the mule which pulled the new invention out of mudholes and sand beds when engine balked and tires subsided.

Rural horizons are being pushed back. The twenty miles that once represented a day's journey in the farmer's little world are now less than an hour's spin.

The broadening experience that travel brings; the development of judgment and decision that automobile driving requires; the spread of mechanical knowledge that car maintenance

MACHINING FLYWHEELS

This machine has a whole battery of cutting apparatus which dresses up half a dozen flywheels at a time.

entails; the demand for initiative and enterprise in those who would own and operate an automobile, are giving to the American people a training the value of which cannot be estimated in dollars and cents.

Many a wise leader of industry has sensed the significance of car ownership by his employees, and is encouraging them to buy homes where houses are detached and where they can own cars. The president of the Baldwin Loco-

THE DISPATCHER'S OFFICE IN AN AUTOMOBILE PLANT

These boards, in the production department of a major plant, control the passage through the factory of material and parts, bringing them together at the right time and showing the status of operations all the way through to the finished product.

WINDING ARMATURES FOR MOTOR-CAR GENERATORS

Until recently it has been necessary to wind armatures with these comparatively simple hand machine. To keep the tension uniform with the constant starting and stopping of the wire reels of the type shown in the left foreground was apparently an unsolvable problem. A new machine has just been perfected, however, which automatically winds the armatures, one girl being able to do the work of four, with none of the strain involved. The wire is drawn on a 15-pound tension.

motive Works has told his men that he wants all of them to have initiative enough to own cars.

ELEVEN OUT OF EVERY THIRTEEN MOTOR CARS IN THE WORLD REGISTERED HERE

What people could appreciate and capitalize the advantage of the motor car so well as those of America? Their wealth is more widely distributed than that of any other nation; their average income is equaled nowhere else on the planet; furthermore, they have an unexcelled genius for quantity production. It is these facts that are responsible for eleven out of every thirteen motor vehicles in the world being operated on American roads, and for twelve out of every thirteen produced in a given period being Yankee-made.

Surveying motor-car registration, we find that South Carolina has more cars than Australia or Argentina; that Kansas has more than France or Germany; that Michigan has more than Great Britain and Ireland.

Indeed, New York, Pennsylvania, New Jersey, and Maryland, with a combined popula-

A VIEW OF CHARLES STREET, BOSTON,
WITH THE COMMON ON THE RIGHT AND THE PUBLIC GARDEN ON THE LEFT
The passing of the day of putting down the tops of touring cars is to be noted wherever cars are parked.

MOTOR TRAFFIC ON FIFTH AVENUE, NORTH OF 42ND STREET, NEW YORK:
A NORMAL SCENE AT ANY HOUR OF THE BUSINESS DAY

"Some 42,000 motor vehicles pass the crossing at Fifth Avenue and 42nd Street every twenty-four hours; 4,500 in a single busy hour is not an unusual occurrence" (see text, page 25).

tion smaller than Poland, and with an aggregate area more limited than New Mexico, have more automobiles in service than the whole world outside of the United States.

Even the District of Columbia has more motor vehicles than Austria, Belgium, Brazil, South Africa, China, Cuba, Czechoslovakia, Denmark, India, Japan, Jugo-Slavia, Mexico, The Netherlands, New Zealand, Norway, Po-land, Portugal, Rumania, Russia, Spain, Sweden, or Switzerland.

In a group of twenty-eight major cities of the country, there are more cars stolen annually, even, than are used in Austria, Belgium, Japan, or Mexico.

The insatiable demand for new cars, in spite of the tremendous number already in service, is disclosed by the fact that many more will

PAINTING WITH COMPRESSED AIR IN A TRACTOR PLANT

By the time the tractor reaches this booth on the assembly line, everything is in place except the wheels, which are put on just beyond the paint booth. Gray paint is sprayed on by compressed air. After the wheels are put on, the line passes through a drying tunnel 110 feet long, in which the temperature is maintained at 150 degrees.

be called into commission this year than were built from the birth of the industry up to the end of 1915.

Available figures indicate that the total car sales for the year will approximate five millions, including two million used vehicles. This means that one family out of every four in the country annually figures in an automobile transaction.

WHEN WILL THE POINT OF SATURATION BE REACHED?

With such facts before them, men naturally pause and wonder how it can be that the long anticipated "point of saturation"—that is, the hour when the country's demand for new cars will be limited to replacements—is not reached.

All the economists have been predicting its arrival for years. A decade and a half ago it was learnedly urged that the wealth of the country could never support more than two hundred thousand new cars a year. A little later it was being said that when the registration reached the five-million mark it would slow down to the slight annual increase required for the growth in population.

But that mark was passed and the expansion continued, with ten millions as the limit beyond which it seemed impossible to go. Today that limit has been exceeded and there are once more many considerations which would seem to indicate that the "point of saturation" is close at hand. Car registration is now up to the point where it is only a million behind the telephone listings of the country, only seven millions behind the total number of families, and even closer than that to the total number of dwellings.

Yet contrary to these considerations, and in spite of the warning from financiers that many people who can't afford them are buying cars, and in the face of the additional fact that 70 per cent of the cars being sold are bought on the deferred-payment plan, the demand goes on unchecked except as affected by seasonal conditions.

A study of Uncle Sam's expense account for motor-car transportation shows that it totals seven billion dollars annually. Men naturally wonder how we can go far beyond that, but they forget that for every dollar added to our national automobile transportation expenses we add several dollars to our national income.

WHO CAN AFFORD AN AUTOMOBILE?

An old-time, long-headed man in the automobile industry has a theory that seems to be the answer to the issue of who can afford to buy a car.

"I get tremendously tired of all this talk about this man and that man not being able to support an automobile," said he. "It's just like the question of whether a given man can afford to get married or not. One man, in whom only his bride has confidence, makes a success of matrimony and life. On the other hand, another man embarks on the matrimonial sea who is regarded as well fixed, and he makes a total failure of his venture."

Many a man is "made" by marriage, and not a few are developed by automobile ownership. But just as matrimony enriches the nation, however much it costs in dollars and cents, so does transportation—and that is what the automobile is.

Many things are happening that promise to postpone our arrival at the "point of saturation," however much the signs indicate its nearness.

FACTORY TESTING OF SPEEDOMETERS

Before being packed, speedometers are given a final test for accuracy by running them at different speeds on a testing machine. This is the last of the 557 inspections given each instrument and its parts in the course of its construction.

DOUBLE-DECKING FLAT FREIGHT CARS FOR BIG MOTOR-CAR SHIPMENTS

Despite the fact that a third of a million carloads of cars were shipped from factories last year, and 75,000 more from assembling plants, and still other thousands by Great Lake steamers, it has been necessary to send many cars to distribution centers in drive-away fleets. One manufacturer maintains a corps of drive-away men, sending the cars out in fleets of ten, each with a captain and a mechanic. Drivers are not allowed to raise the hoods of their cars and must keep their assigned positions in the fleet. The speed is held down to 25 miles an hour.

Graphs of prices and production show that price reduction has always served to widen the demand. Every fifty dollars' reduction in selling price opens up, according to the graphs, a new field of a million prospects.

The deferred-payment plan also widened the market tremendously for all cars, and now the much-discussed "five dollars down and five a week" scheme of the Ford Motor Company is enrolling hundreds of thousands of new customers.

But that plan, it seems, is not exactly what on its face it appears to be. The dealer is to use his judgment as to how many months these payments will have to continue before the customer gets his car. If the latter convinces him of his ability to go on paying, the car will be delivered after thirty weeks. Otherwise, the whole sum, even, may be required before delivery is made, and by that time the buyer will have had a pretty good lesson in thrift.

HUMAN EFFICIENCY AND THE AUTOMOBILE

A questionnaire sent out to thousands of automobile owners at random all over the coun-

THE LAKE CRESCENT ROAD, AMONG THE FINE FIRS OF THE STATE OF WASHINGTON

A proposition is now being advocated to give the North Coast people a bridge entrance into San Francisco. A territory as large as the State of Rhode Island would thus be thrown open to settlement. It is proposed to charge a bridge toll of $1.18 per car and 15 cents per passenger or pedestrian. The bridge would be about 7,500 feet long. In 1921, 200,000 cars were handled on the Golden Gate ferry.

ARRIVING BY MOTOR FOR THE RUBIDOUX EASTER SERVICE, RIVERSIDE, CALIFORNIA

try throws some light on the specific increase in efficiency that the motor car brings to its possessor. The summing up of the answers shows a 56.7 per cent increase in working capacity. Applied to the millions of car-owners, this would represent the equivalent of adding nearly seven million new workers to the nation's productive forces.

The promotion of efficiency in those who own cars is only the beginning of the direct returns that the industry makes in balancing the tremendous expenditure for automobile transportation. It gives direct employment to more than a million men and indirect to two or three times as many. It buys the major portion of the country's plate glass, a vast share of its iron and steel, most of its aluminum, much of its leather. It gives the railroads much more freight to haul than it takes from them.

It has sent hundreds of thousands of people into the suburbs, where rents are cheaper and living conditions better, and where the savings in rent offset the car's maintenance costs, leaving the better living conditions as dividends.

Yet the direct contributions to national prosperity are small compared with the indirect contributions briefly referred to above—the expanding city and the narrowing countryside. What stories the rusty little cars parked around the rural high school could tell of boys and girls who will finish their secondary education, when their parents never got beyond the sixth grade!

Before the coming of the motor car, the farmer who was not up at five in the morning or who had left the field before sundown in the evening was accounted a shiftless tiller of the soil. From seven to seven in the field, with his morning and evening chores before and after, was his routine.

HOME OWNERSHIP INCREASES WITH CAR REGISTRATION

That he is now released from such a grind; that his family is coming into its normal share of diversion and recreation; that he can provide his children with opportunities that fate hitherto denied him, is due mainly to the motor car and the train of advantages it has brought him. The farm bureau, the rural woman's club, the parent-teacher association, are but a few evidences of his intellectual emancipation. In

HANGING ON BEHIND: THROUGH A FORD IN ROCK CREEK PARK, WASHINGTON, D. C.

A Michigan lumberman invented the modern spark plug; a Russian Jew, the demountable rim; a mid-western engineer, the orthodox self-starter; and a New England Yankee, the antiskid chain—a quartet of inventions that has been a major factor in the development of motoring in America.

Pennsylvania 65 per cent of the farmers own motor cars, and other States show similar percentages.

When will the point of saturation be reached, in the light of such direct and indirect returns, and in view of the fact that fewer deferred-payment buyers default on their cars than on household furniture; that definite statistics show home ownership increasing with motor- car registration; that national income increases as automotive transportation outgo swells?

Measured by California's present ratio of car-owners to population, it will not be reached until the present registration of the country is doubled.

Yet even California has not settled down to replacements. Measured by Indiana's existing ratio, the ultimate registration of the country would reach eighteen millions, but Indiana still shows herself far on the sunny side of saturation.

Those whose past predictions have been most nearly justified by the trend of events are making new predictions to-day, and these are that the point of saturation will not be economic, but rather physical. The congestion in the big cities is fast growing so great as to keep

HEAVY GOING IN THE WAKE OF A RAINSTORM
IN THE CEDAR BREAKS REGION OF SOUTHERN UTAH

It is estimated by the National Motorists' Association that two and a half million car-owners annually take to the roads of the country for a vacation, and this number represents about ten million tourists.

AT THE FOOT OF YOSEMITE FALLS: YOSEMITE NATIONAL PARK

It is only a little more than twenty-five years ago that the first sale of an automobile was made in this country. The National Motorists Association estimates that more than 2,500,000 car owners will this year use the automobile highways in visiting America's many points of interest.

A COMPLETED STRETCH OF PLANK ROAD OVER THE CALIFORNIA DESERT

Note the turnout in the left foreground. These are built at frequent intervals. Such a road would not be practical where there was excessive shifting of sand dunes.

thousands of motorists out of the down-town districts.

BIG CITY TRAFFIC PROBLEMS

With all the traffic officers and signal systems, the task of handling the everflowing stream of motor cars and trucks grows apace. Some 42,000 motor vehicles pass the crossing at Fifth Avenue and Forty-second Street in New York every twenty-four hours; 4,500 in a single busy hour is not an unusual occurrence.

The block-signal system on Fifth Avenue, with traffic moving in a series of stops and starts, controlled from a central tower, has accomplished much, but even it is destined to prove inadequate. Boulevard traffic regulation, based on the Fifth Avenue practice, has also helped

in many cities, but here again inadequacy is only a few years away.

Propositions are now coming from the foremost authorities for the establishment of express streets, where cars will move at rates of from forty to fifty miles an hour, and where gates will be established at intersections, just as at railway crossings. Commissioner Harriss, of New York, says that New York needs three north-and-south highways of this character, with traffic moving on each of them in three parallel lines in both directions. These streets, he says, will have to be four hundred feet wide and elevated in special instances.

Chicago is installing a synchronized traffic-control system similar to that now in operation in New York. This system of towers will extend south on Michigan Boulevard from Randolph Street, with the master tower at Jackson.

So great is the congestion in the famous Loop District in Chicago that proposals are being made to take all pedestrians off of the street level and to provide second-story sidewalks for them. The streets could then be widened to the building lines, almost doubling their present curb-to-curb width, and the sidewalks would be reached by stairways, ramps, and elevators. Vehicular and pedestrian traffic, each out of the way of the other, could move twice as fast as now and many times more safely.

THE OREGON STATE MOTOR ASSOCIATION
PLANS TO TAKE OREGON SCENERY ABROAD

The back of the Association's pathfinder car is being painted with a scene showing Mt. Hood, with the city of Portland in the foreground.

MOTOR TRUCKS PROTECT THE PUBLIC DURING STREET-CAR STRIKES

In many cities motor cars have helped the public get down town when the street-car service has been interrupted.

HAULING PULP WOOD IN THE MAINE WOODS

By combining truck, tractor, and bob-sled, the Maine lumbermen have found a practical way to move pulp wood, used in the manufacture of paper, over the ice and snow in winter.

STUDENTS LEAVING THE PINE LEVEL, ALABAMA, JUNIOR HIGH SCHOOL

NOW COMES THE TRAVELING GROCERY

A Cincinnati grocer decided to try a "help yourself and pay as you leave" store on wheels. He found the venture so profitable that he proposes to add other cars to his fleet.

It is pointed out that such a plan would give two display window stories instead of one, and that the thousands of people who now avoid the Loop District because of its congestion would come back to trade there, their reclaimed business being large enough to more than compen-

A PREACHER AND HIS PERIPATETIC PULPIT

A Brooklyn clergyman decided to fulfill literally the admonition to "go out into the highways." His traveling chapel has stained-glass windows, a small organ, and a steeple that can be lowered to permit passage into a garage.

sate the property owners for the cost of the change.

The day may not be so far in the distance when the horse-drawn vehicle will be legislated off the crowded city thoroughfares, to lessen congestion, just as heavy traffic has been banished from the boulevards to protect the motoring public. Likewise, the day will inevitably come when truck traffic will be separated

from passenger-car traffic on the busier highways through the countryside, just as is now the case on the fine Roosevelt Boulevard out of Philadelphia.

But whenever the point of saturation is reached, and by whatever route, it will not come before all manufacturing facilities available today will be kept busy making replacements. The average life of a motor car is six years. If

THE MORNING TOILET ON TOUR

Camping outfits of many kinds and degrees of comfort are on the market to-day, and the demand for them is showing a remarkable increase with each succeeding tourist season.

18,000,000 cars shall prove the limit, replacement requirements will call for three millions a year, which represent the present annual production.

THE AUTOMOBILE
AN EFFICIENT MECHANISM

There is little wonder that the automobile has caught the imagination of the American people. A race of individualists, the sense of power to go where they will, in their own way, has a deep appeal. Further than that, a mechanically minded people, they find a thrill in the possession of a mechanism whose purring motor bowls them along the highways at a pace that exhilarates and brings a change of scene every minute. They have a sort of subconscious reverence for its mechanical merit.

And well they may! Consider what a present-day model automobile is. Its engine might be likened to a Gattling gun capable of propelling itself a mile a minute and, if it be a "six," of firing nine thousand shots a minute in doing so, without noise, undue heat, or disturbing wear, but rather with a smooth hum or a peaceful purr that is music to the ear of the motorist. A "four," even at twenty miles per hour, fires two thousand shots a minute.

The crankshaft must do three thousand full turns in the average car to carry it a mile, and each piston must make six thousand trips start his car and light his path. It gives him a clutch that lets him make or break the power between his engine and his car at will and in a twinkling; a gearshift that lets him choose between power and speed and makes the change in a moment; brakes that give him complete control of a ton and a half vehicle with a slight pressure of the foot or a light pull of the hand. It furnishes him with tires made of a rubber composition nearly three times as durable as leather and fully three times as resistant to a sand blast as iron.

Compared with any previous instrument of transportation, the automobile is a wonderful device. A railroad engine, made to run over the smoothest roadbed in the world and with comparatively slow-moving parts, must be overhauled at the end of every run. On the other hand, given gas and oil, grease and water, in proper quantities, the "trusty old bus" will hum along for two hundred miles a day, willing to give you, if it is a "six," more than half a million flywheel revolutions, nearly two million sparks, and more than seven million piston stops and starts, and be ready to repeat the performance on the morrow and many other morrows.

BOOKS COME BY MOTOR TO GLADDEN THE LIVES
OF THE COUNTRY CHILDREN

Many counties are introducing a motorized circulating library service for the rural districts.

through its cylinder, with a stop between each of them, in making that mile. At sixty miles you ask each valve to open, admit the live, or discharge the dead gas, and close again, in 1/200 of a second. And they are expected to do it with clockwork regularity.

The car also brings to its owner an individual light-and-power plant with which he may

PROBLEMS THAT REMAIN TO BE SOLVED

Yet, far as our automotive engineers have gone in making a dependable, fool-proof, vibration-defying, long-lasting motor car, they realize that much distance remains yet to be traveled before the goal of excellence they are striving for can be reached.

To begin with, our engines to-day deliver us only ten cents' worth of power for every dollar's worth of gas they burn. Their pistons must travel twenty inches, on the basis of one explosion to every four strokes, to deliver five inches of push to their load.

Likewise, our cars ask us to move from 400 to 5,000 pounds of dead weight per person carried, depending on whether they be loaded "flivvers" or big sedans with only the owner inside. These and other items in the present car's make-up stand as a perpetual challenge to the automotive engineer, and he is addressing himself vigorously to the task of correcting them.

RUNNING DOWN THE "KNOCK"

When cars were first made, the builders simply bored holes in blocks, put pistons in them, and had engines. They had only a general idea of what happens when a spark is applied to a compressed charge of gas in an engine cylinder. When the explosion took place under high compression, there came a knock that seriously reduced the engine's efficiency. All sorts of explanations for this knock were offered.

Then Mr. C. F. Kettering and his associates of the General Motors Research Laboratories decided to look into cylinders and see what does actually happen when a spark ignites a charge of gas.

They built a glass engine, and through its walls were able to see what occurred. They found that in an explosion under high compression there is a secondary detonation whose energy waves move seventy times as fast as those of the primary explosion. It is the conflict of these two series of energy waves that makes the power-destroying "knock."

How to overcome this detonation became the next problem. The whole list of elements and compounds known to the laboratory was gone over and every one that offered any hope was tested. It was finally found that by adding tetra ethyl lead and a second compound in the proportion of about five thimblefuls to the gallon the secondary detonation was entirely avoided, and smooth running, even under the high compression beyond the control of a retarded spark, was made possible.

It has been found that the new combination makes five gallons of gasoline do the work of six, and the engineers assert that by reducing the size of the cylinder and the stroke of the piston it will be possible to produce higher-speed engines that will more than double the present mileage obtained from a gallon of gas.

On the other hand, there are engineers who say that while this will make possible the saving in gas, it will result in a corresponding wear on cylinder walls by the increased distance the pistons must travel to produce a mile of transportation.

The reduction of weight in cars is a very important item in the future plans of automobile design. One noted manufacturer says that unnecessary weight is as useless in a car as a cockade on a coachman's hat, if not more so, since the cockade at least serves the purpose of identification. The reduction of weight means smaller motors, lighter axles, and less cumbersome frames and running gear, all of which promise less expensive tires and decreasing operating costs.

OVERCOMING THE NECESSITY OF WATER-COOLING

One of the new departures in engine design that serves to reduce weight is the substitution of copper-cooling for water-cooling. The function of water in an automobile engine is to carry the heat from the cylinders to the radiator cells, where it is released by radiation.

For a long time, at least one manufacturer has been able to produce an air-cooled engine, with iron fins surrounding the cylinders, that has stood up well in every-day service. The engineering textbooks all declare that it is impossible to fuse copper and iron in a commercial way. However, at least two manufacturers have succeeded in doing so, and two

A MOTORIZED TYPEWRITER SALES SERVICE

A Bloomington, Illinois, typewriter agency decided to send its salesmen on the road with a full line of samples. A specially designed automobile body was installed, and now the typewriter store travels from town to town and from office to office. Each machine is mounted on a board that can be pulled out and made to serve as a demonstration desk.

MINIATURE "TWIN-LEG" SEDAN

A Boston mechanic built his son a toy automobile with everything orthodox save an engine. The young motorist insisted on finding a "cop" who would "arrest" him.

cars are now on the market with copper cylinder jackets which claim to give radiation efficiency fully up to the standard of the modern water-cooled system.

Copper, being much more efficient as a heat-radiating medium than iron, makes an ideal substitute for water, eliminating radiator repairs, freezing dangers, etc. The copper-cooled engine weighs less by about 130 pounds than a water-cooled engine of similar horsepower and cooling efficiency.

ANTI-FRICTION BEARINGS

One of the prime causes of short life in motor cars is neglect in the matter of lubrication. Owners of fleets of cars, notably some of the taxicab companies, get from 200,000 to 300,000 miles out of a machine. The owner of an individual car considers that he has done well when his odometer registers 50,000 miles. His neglect of lubrication is more frequently responsible than any other one item for his low mileage.

The General Motors Research Corporation has been working on the task of producing a nonfriction bearing, and demonstrations at Dayton point to complete success. Instead of melting the metal and molding the molten fluid, it is powdered, put into the mold in that form, and subjected to heat. The alloy has a lower melting point than the steel itself and thus is made a homogeneous part of the material. When taken out of the furnace, the bearing has a certain porosity not present in bearings molded in the orthodox manner. It is capable of absorbing a certain percentage of its weight in lubricants.

Under dynamometer tests these bearings have been run at 2,000 revolutions per minute, which is equivalent to a speed of the crankshaft of a car running 40 miles an hour. Although told that they had been running for 3,600 and 3,700 hours without stop, they were still cool enough for me to bear my hand on them when I examined them.

With frictionless bearings, burned-out bushings will probably be a thing of the past.

SEEING THE COUNTRY GYPSY FASHION

This bungalow car, fitted with the comforts of a modern apartment, including electric lights and plumbing and a convertible living and bed room, has brought happiness to a motor-minded family. Even the driver's seat can be converted into an upper and lower berth.

A GROUP OF CHILDREN FROM SIX STATES
FORMING A HAPPY CIRCLE IN OVERLAND PARK CAMP GROUNDS, DENVER, COLORADO

Hundreds of cities and towns have provided camps for tourists, most of them equipped with electric lights, kitchens and sanitary conveniences, and provided with police protection. One Missouri town of 7,000 inhabitants recently made a count. Its citizens welcomed 23,520 cars, carrying 100,000 passengers, during the touring season. More than 3,000 cars, carrying 12,000 passengers, stopped at the town's free camping site.

The antifriction element in them will be used mainly to counteract neglect. It will be the savings-account funds of car operation—not to be drawn on except in emergency.

THE STATUS OF STEEL BODIES

Engineers predict that the automobile bodies of the future in all quantity-production cars will be steel. Not only does metal construction reduce the time required for the completion of a sedan body from more than one hundred days to less than two, but it also makes a more lasting job.

Instead of glue and screws with which a wooden body is put together, electric welding and rivets are used, which make for permanency. It is the difference between the modern all-steel Pullman car and the old-fashioned coach of wood construction.

Baked-on enamel, applied in a few hours, if correctly put on, shows much more durability than the best hand-painting, which requires eighteen days or more. The enamel does not deteriorate, but, owing to atmospheric and temperature conditions, merely collects a residue of blue scum that is readily removed with a proper polish. A report of an enamel job done in 1914 was made at a recent meeting of a branch of the Society of Automotive Engineers. Good care had been taken of the car; it had been polished and kept clean, and in 1922 appeared practically as new.

MEETING THE DEMAND
FOR ACCESSIBILITY

The motorist of the future will demand accessibility of parts. The important thing with taxicab companies is the keeping of their vehicles out of the shop and in the streets. There-fore, accessibility of parts is a sort of religion with the leading manufacturers of taxicabs.

Bolts and nuts must be so located as to insure ease and rapidity in removal or installation, and parts must be quickly exchangeable.

So thoroughly has the construction of a standard type of cab been simplified that twenty minutes is now the time allowed for the replacing of a spring, forty minutes for the removal of an engine, and fifty minutes for the reinstallation of an engine.

The introduction of the flat rate in service charges, whereby each operation is done at a factory-fixed rate, is destined to hasten the simplification of car design, for the manufacturer who can make a car simpler for the repair man than his competitor can give a lower rate for service, and this will be one of the standards by which the future buyer will determine who will make his next car.

A leading taxicab manufacturing company, with its vast fleet of cars in operation and its detailed cost-keeping system for car operation, is doing much to guide the industry toward the production of cars whose maintenance costs will be lower.

THE ADVANTAGES
OF SUPER-SIZED TIRES

It has been found that vibration is the worst enemy of an automobile, and this evil has been attacked from many angles.

One line of investigation has been in the reduction of tire-inflation pressure. In pursuing this investigation it has been found that by the further extension of the oversized tire principle, inflation can be reduced from the sixty or eighty pounds pressure to thirty and forty pounds.

A WEEK-END ALONGSIDE ONE OF NEW YORK'S STATE HIGHWAYS

BUYING PEACHES ON A NEW YORK STATE HIGHWAY

Motorists in New York and New England find everything, from apples and peaches to eggs and jellies, offered for sale by the roadside; and the prices are usually surprisingly low.

One taxicab company is having tires made with wider treads. This has been carried so far that some of the tires look like big, fat sausages. But the reduction of vibration due to their softness has shown amazing results in cost of car upkeep and even in car life. The tires are built with thinner walls, and through their ability to take the minor shocks of the road more easily, their mileage is lengthened to such a degree as to compensate for their higher cost, leaving both the car protection and ridability as dividends on the investment.

Skidding is reduced to a minimum with these super-sized tires, brake control is made more complete, and muddy roads are robbed of many of their terrors. Steering is not noticeably more difficult at ordinary speeds, though admittedly it is somewhat harder at slow speeds, as is the turning of the front wheels when the car is standing still.

The coming of the super-sized tire will result in a smaller wheel—a wheel, indeed, not much larger than some of the brake drums now in use. It may mean a slight lengthening of the axles in order to maintain the present turning radius, though, on the other hand, it may be decided to concede a little in turning radius in order to maintain the present axle-length.

THE REMAINS OF A RAIDED STILL ABOARD A FAITHFUL "FLIVVER"

There is a Ford driver born every thirteen seconds to keep pace with the output of the automobile plants at River Rouge and Highland Park.

A FLEET OF TRUCKS ON THE COURTHOUSE PLAZA
IN BALTIMORE EN ROUTE FROM DETROIT TO FRANCE

FOUR-WHEEL BRAKES
A NEW DEPARTURE

With the increasing use of automobiles increased control of the individual car is demanded. To be able to bring a car more quickly to a standstill sometimes means the avoidance of an accident. Four-wheel brakes are beginning to make their appearance in this country, and have been found to cut practically in half the distance required for bringing a moving car to a stop. Many manufacturers believe, however, that the super-sized tires will give the requisite braking efficiency without resorting to four-wheel brakes.

WHO SETS THE FASHIONS
IN MOTOR-CAR DESIGN?

Automotive engineers are giving more and more attention to what they call the passenger accommodations—everything above the chassis. While the body and its accessories have little to do with the mechanical merit of the car, they have a vast deal to do with the sale demand.

And this, in turn, throws some light on the question of who sets motordom's fashions. A manufacturer making an assembled car on a small scale brings out something new in body design—say, a new sport model. It has various little touches that please the eye and promote the comfort of the passenger.

When it goes before the public, many buyers forget the fact that the value of a motor car is mainly in the chassis, and make a selection without considering that phase of the subject.

Then the staid manufacturer of a staple chassis that has stood the test of years finds that, if the new types are not to undermine his sales, he must meet the competition, and so he sets

about to do so, with the result that a new fashion becomes a settled part of the industry.

WHEN MILADY SETS THE PACE FOR EASE AND SAFETY

Statistics have been gathered which show that the ladies have an unsuspected voice in the selection of the family motor car. This is causing most manufacturers to cater to their tastes with great care.

One company puts a thermos bottle in as standard equipment. Another makes his oil-draining system so easy of operation that a woman can drain the crank case without difficulty. Another groups the instrument-board

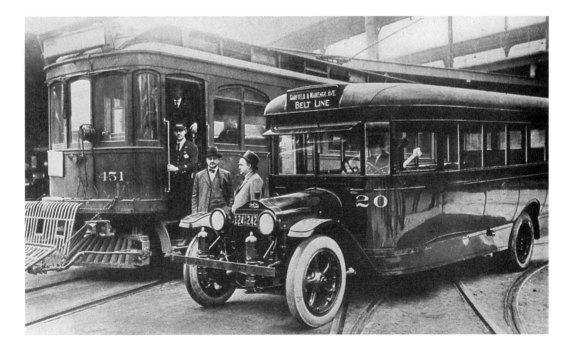

A MODERN MOTOR BUS AND A CAR OF THE TRACTION LINE IT SERVES

Sixty electric lines are now using motor busses to supplement their service. They serve admirably in new territory as feeders to established street-car and interurban traction lines.

equipment under one glass, so that the board can be kept looking like new.

Still another puts on an improved type of brake-equalizer, so as to insure, in a measure at least, Milady driver against skidding. Gear shifting and clutch operation have been made easier to catch her eye. Accelerator pedals have been redesigned, so that they function equally well with high-heeled dress boots and low-heeled sport shoes. Spark and gas control levers on the steering wheel are being redesigned to obviate the danger of feminine fingers being caught between the control sectors and the steering-wheel spokes when turning corners, and to lessen the risk of stray ends of the woman driver's finery being torn in the control mechanism as she drives to the next bridge party.

One manufacturer provides for automatic recranking in case she stalls her engine and another takes steps to insure a better mixture in a cold engine or in a sudden acceleration of the motor.

TAKING YOUR BED WITH YOU

In an attempt to capitalize America's love for camping out, one car builder has announced a model in which the Pullman berth idea is copied. Press a button and the back of the front seat drops down. Reverse the cushion on the rear seat, and lo! you have a bed inside your car! Tents eliminated, you are ready to make your bed wherever night overtakes you—by a babbling brook, under a fine willow, or wherever fancy dictates.

The maker of a standard, medium-priced car was asked what he thought would be the future trend of car design for the masses. He replied that his factory was working toward the time when it would put out a model weighing about 1,800 pounds and accommodating four instead of five passengers.

In no other field does one find such close coöperation as in the motor-car industry. The manufacturers in the early days were forced to unite for the purpose of fighting hostile legislation and for making the American public motor-minded. They found that they could make a better market for their individual cars by teamwork with their competitors in selling the car idea. They learned that their success was linked with their competitors' success.

"COÖPERATIVE COMPETITION"

So "coöperative competition" became their watchword. Young, virile men with imagination made this policy a tremendous success, so much so that they agreed among themselves to form a pool of ideas. In this pool there are about 500 patents, and every member of the National Automobile Chamber of Commerce, which includes practically all the leading manufacturers, voluntarily agrees to let every other member use any or all of the features of construction and equipment owned by them individually without the payment of royalties or other compensation. They hold that the better service all cars render the greater will be the demand for their own.

One of the interesting organizations within the industry is the Society of Automotive Engineers. Its main purpose, when organized, was to promote standardization among manufacturers, but it has found its principal continuing mission to be that of a research body serving as a clearing house in automotive engineering and design development.

Standardization has been a big task. The fixing of metal standards has assured a consistent and dependable product to the discomfi-

ARMY TRUCKS AT CAMP HOLABIRD, BALTIMORE, MARYLAND

The truck on the right is the regulation army truck widely used by our Expeditionary Forces in France. In the middle is the new six-wheel truck recently devised (see page 48). By the use of oversized tires, the ratio of weight per square inch on the road surface is reduced from 7 to 2½. The truck at the left is also a new design, built at Camp Holabird and having a four-wheel drive. This truck will go almost anywhere that a caterpillar tractor can operate, and some places it cannot, and at the same time it has a high road efficiency.

ture of foreign manufacturers. Sizes in wheels and cotterpins, threading of spark plugs, details of tire fastenings, angles of valve-seating, and scores of other items that could be made to fit all cars without detracting in the slightest degree from the engineering originality in car construction that differentiates one car from another, have been standardized, and this standardization lies at the base of quantity production, which, in its turn, plays a fundamental part in American supremacy in the automobile field.

It was found that one company making lock washers for the automobile manufacturers was obliged to make 800 different kinds of washers for bolts ranging from three-sixteenths to one-fourth of an inch in diameter.

It was likewise discovered that the automobile manufacturers were using 1,600 different sizes of steel tubing. Standardization has reduced the number of sizes of washers and tubing to a minimum, with saving in cost of manufacture, reduction of inventory, and convenience to the public.

HOW AUTOMOBILE RACING GIVES THE PUBLIC BETTER CARS

In the early days automobile racing was indulged in for the purpose of showing that cars could get over the road at all, and such races as that sponsored by newspapers in 1895 seem ludicrous at this distance.

Later, people began to think of speed. They wanted cars that could make thirty miles an hour, and the car that showed the most speed was the one that found the readiest sale.

In one of these races for advertising purposes, Henry Ford himself took part in a contraption he called the "Arrow." He undertook to run it a mile straightaway over the ice. The ice looked smooth, but when he got up speed he found it was covered with fissures. To call off the race would be throwing his advertising into reverse gear. So, in his words, "I let the old 'Arrow' out. At every fissure the car leaped into the air. I never knew how it was coming down. When I wasn't in the air, I was skidding, but somehow I stayed top side up and on the course."

TEN OF A KIND TAKING THE TWIN PEAKS' GRADE ON HIGH AT SAN FRANCISCO

A San Francisco distributor decided to show the world what his cars could do on heart-breaking hills. Ten owners, one a woman, came to the scratch at the foot of the hill and not a gear was shifted after the start. The power of the American-built motor represents an outstanding engineering achievement.

DRIFTING DOWN THE MOUNTAIN SIDE ON THE PIKES PEAK HIGHWAY

In no other way is the relegation of the horse from the streets and highways of the country more strikingly attested than in the decadence of the horse-drawn-vehicle industry. In 1914 the output of horse-drawn vehicles was valued at $131,000,000. In 1921 it had declined to $42,000,000—a slump of 67.8 per cent in seven years.

Some years later road racing came into vogue, and it did a vast deal in the development of motors, the evolution of spring design, the perfection of ignition, and the solution of lubrication problems.

After the road races came the reliability runs, made under conditions that found the weak spots in the stock cars put under test, and they, in turn, served to shake down engineering standards to the level of dependability.

But later came the speedway races. To them came the best ideas the ablest engineers in the world could evolve, to be put to the grueling tests that only a speedway race can set up. The first speedway built was at Indianapolis, with James A. Allison, A. C. Newby, and Carl G. Fisher as the moving spirits in its construction.

The roadbed was built of earth, like a country highway, but after the first test of 500 miles the conditions were found to be dangerous and unsatisfactory, and straightway it was rebuilt of brick and made to simulate street conditions. No car ever entered one of the races thereafter and went through the grueling test without revealing its weak points.

Every automotive engineer in the profession seeks to know as fully what to avoid as what to incorporate in his future models. The result has been that these terrific tests at Indianapolis have always brought the engineering talent of the country together.

Under the lessons learned there—and obtainable in no other manner, since bench tests cannot develop road conditions—cylinder displacement has been reduced, fuel economy has been evolved, and safety has been forged into every element of your motor car and mine on the mighty anvil of a speedway and under the powerful hammer of high speed. Harmony, bal-ance, dependability, tire mileage, and sturdiness have come from the flaming forge of a hundred miles an hour (see illustrations, pp. 3 and 4).

THE ROMANCE
OF QUANTITY PRODUCTION

Quantity production is, after all, the foundation stone upon which rests the success of the automotive industry. Without it motor cars would certainly be beyond the means of millions of persons who now own them. In the early days they were largely made by hand. Today the use of a paint brush or a pair of spanners, the movement of a lever, or the holding of an electric wrench represents about the limit of handwork in motor-car manufacture. That precision tools are superior to human senses in automobile making has been strikingly demonstrated.

CLIPPING MINUTES IN MOTOR MAKING

In the early days the material for the assembly of a car was simply dumped together in a space on the floor where the automobile was to be set up. Then the Ford Motor Company thought to try out the overhead trolley system used by the Chicago packers and a division of labor.

One man could assemble a flywheel magneto in twenty minutes. When the moving line was installed and divided into twenty-nine operations, the time was cut down to less than fourteen minutes. By raising the height of the line eight inches, so as to save stooping, the time was reduced to seven minutes. Other experiments reduced the time to five minutes.

In 1913, 9 hours and 54 minutes were required to assemble a motor in the Ford plant.

MOTORIZED TRANSPORT IN THE UNITED STATES ARMY

Six months later the time had been reduced to 5 hours and 56 minutes.

By early methods 12 hours and 28 minutes was the time required to assemble a chassis. Then the idea was evolved of towing the chassis down a 250-foot line with a rope attached to a windlass. Six assemblers walked down the line, picking up parts from various piles and attaching them as the car moved. This speeded up the assembly to 5 hours and 50 minutes. By placing the work waist-high and bringing the speed of the conveyor to the most effective point, the time of assembly was reduced to 1 hour and 33 minutes.

It was quite a task to determine at what speed each conveyor should move so as to give each workman ample time to do his bit properly and yet economize every second. The flywheel magneto assembly line was tried at sixty feet a minute, and that proved too fast. Eighteen feet per minute proved too slow. Forty-four feet finally proved to be the correct velocity.

A SECTION OF THE STORM KING HIGHWAY
BETWEEN CORNWALL AND WEST POINT, NEW YORK

It is such scenery as this that has drawn millions of motorists and their families into the great American out-of-doors and brought rejuvenation to tired nerves and sluggish bodies.

A NEW SIX-WHEEL TRUCK
DESIGNED BY THE QUARTERMASTER'S DEPARTMENT, U. S. A., AT CAMP HOLABIRD

This picture shows the flexibility of the truck construction of the new six-wheel type the army is developing. The one-foot rule shows the height of the block on which the one wheel rests. The block on the opposite side is six inches high. The four-wheel rear construction shown here can be built for the Government at practically the same expense as the orthodox two-wheel single-axle construction.

In a leading plant the chassis assembly line moves at six feet per minute and has forty-five operations. The first man puts on the mudguard brackets, the motor arrives in the tenth stage, and so on. Some men do only one or two small operations. The man who places a part does not fasten it; the man who puts in a bolt does not put on the nut; the man who puts on the nut does not tighten it.

On operation No. 34 the motor gets its gas, having received its oil earlier. At station No. 44 the radiator is filled with water, and at No. 45 a button is pressed, a pair of rollers in the floor under the rear wheels begins to revolve rapidly, the wheels spin, the engine turns over, and the car glides away under its own power with a driver at the wheel.

Going back a little, the molding in the foundry is all done by machinery. A line is adapted to the making of a single type of casting. In the casting of the engine block there are three lines with a capacity of 5,000 blocks every eight hours, or 15,000 when working three shifts a day. The making of the molds and cores and the packing of the cores are all done while the line moves. At another point the molten metal is poured, and by the time the mold reaches the end of its journey, the casting is cool enough to start on its automatic way to cleaning, machining, and assembly.

UNPRODUCTIVE STEPS ELIMINATED

The piston and connecting-rod assembly is another illustration of the elimination of lost motion in the industry. Under the old plan a man assembled twenty pistons and rods an hour, and subdivision of work didn't seem to promise much saving.

The workman pushed the pin out of the piston, oiled it, slipped the rod in place, replaced the pin, tightened one screw and opened another.

Then came a foreman with a stopwatch. He found that four hours out of every nine were spent taking steps. He subdivided the work into three operations, eliminated unproductive stepping, and now there are 46 pistons assembled per man-hour.

Painting the rear axle was an operation that took two men several minutes; new machinery was devised, and now it is a thirteen-second job for one man.

With its ninety-five tubes, a radiator, even on a Ford, is a rather complex affair. Fitting and

EVEN THE MOUNTAIN COTTAGE FEELS THE TOUCH OF THE AUTOMOBILE

Washington County, Maryland, sends its free library service up into the foothills of the mountains to carry the benediction of books to the poor.

MOTORING THROUGH THE FAMOUS WAWONA TUNNEL TREE,
MARIPOSA GROVE, CALIFORNIA

When Carl G. Fisher suggested the Lincoln Highway and Henry B. Joy sponsored it, they started a development that has done a vast service in opening up the national parks to the American motoring public and to the
general cause of good roads. Roy D. Chapin followed their lead and established a scholarship in highway engineering at the University of Michigan—an idea that other universities have adopted.

soldering these tubes by hand was a long operation, requiring many skilled men. Now a machine is in use which can make 1,200 radiator cores in eight hours, the soldering being done by moving the radiator through a furnace on a metal conveyor, which entirely eliminates the tinsmith.

SUGGESTIONS
FROM THE RANKS

Suggestions come from everywhere in the average quantity production automobile factory, and especially from the ranks. In one plant a Polish workman who could speak no English found that if the tool in his machine were set at a different angle it would wear longer. That discovery saved thousands of dollars in tool-grinding. Another, running a drill press, rigged up a little fixture to save handling after drilling. Tens of thousands of dollars are saved annually by it.

A proposal that castings be taken from the foundry to the machine shop on an overhead conveyor saved seventy men in the transport division.

Seventeen men were required, when production was much smaller than now, to remove burrs from gears. A mechanic roughly designed a machine to do the work. It was perfected, and now four men have several times the output of seventeen, and none of them works as hard as any of their predecessors.

Another man suggested a welded rod instead of a solid one in the chassis, and the resultant economy meant more than half a million dollars a year in this plant. An improvement in heat-treating camshafts reduced the need of shaft straighteners from 37 to 8, although production has nearly doubled.

THE STORY OF THE
GEAR-WHEEL DIPPER

Does the reduction of the intricacy of the work a man performs deaden his initiative or reduce the value of his work to the industry? Many people have asked that question.

In one factory I visited, perhaps the most monotonous task is that of a man who picks up a gear with a steel hook, shakes it in a vat of oil, and then places it in a basket. The monotony of the motion required never varies, and is done without either muscular energy or mental activity. He has done that same job for eight years and has refused offers of promotion. But he has saved $40,000, owns his own home, and drives his own car. It is said that a thorough study has not revealed in that factory a single case of a man's mind being twisted or deadened by such repetitive work.

As to taking skill out of the industry, it is pointed out that, rather, it makes the unskilled laborer partner of the skilled engineer, enabling him, with a mechanism designed by the engineer, to do a job commanding twice the pay he could get without the machine.

LITTLE ECONOMIES
THAT MAKE BIG PROFITS

The old-time tool-sharpener was an expert judge of heat temperatures, but his was a hit-or-miss operation. Now the man who heat-treats steel in an automobile factory has nothing to do with the heat. He never sees the pyrometer that tells when the necessary degree of temperature is reached. Colored electric lights are automatically switched on to tell him when to remove the steel.

Even the "flivver" type of car has about 5,000 parts, counting screws, nuts, and all, and assembly on a quantity production basis must

FIGHTING A CHEMICAL WAREHOUSE FIRE
IN NEW YORK WITH MOTORIZED APPARATUS

The fine spectacle of dashing fire horses is rapidly disappearing. Many of the major cities have completely motorized their fire-fighting equipment. Not long ago the last of Chicago's horse-drawn fire apparatus was discarded, the occasion being made a ceremonial one. A box a short distance from the station was pulled to start the four horses on their last run; after they had left, the new motor equipment was driven in. The efficiency of fire apparatus involves speed and convenience in reaching a fire. Breakage due to rapid runs and the additional hazards of bad pavements and crowded streets result in the necessity for adequate repair departments. New York maintains well-equipped shops where not only worn and damaged apparatus is repaired, but new apparatus is given careful and practical tests before purchase.

THE INTERIOR OF THE MACHINE SHOP OF A BIG TRACTOR PLANT

Quantity production is becoming as marked in tractor plants as in automobile factories. The Iowa State Agricultural College has found that it costs $100 a year to keep a farm horse, and that the average horse works 723 hours. A tractor will do the work of six horses, to say nothing of the human labor saved.

be nicely worked out in every plant. A shortage in a single type lock washer or bolt would tie up the whole line; so the flow of parts must always be constant and dependable.

When it is remembered that the saving of a single cent on each car's production cost means nearly $20,000 a year in the case of the Ford, and $5,000 in the case of the Chevrolet, it can be seen what large prizes small economies win in big factories.

In one plant, the sweepings alone represent a saving of more than half a million dollars annually, and the elimination of a single style of bolt means another half million. Making transmissions in the factory, instead of buying them, saves nearly $20,000,000 a year.

To see a big blast furnace tapped, to watch its white-hot stream of molten iron flow off into giant 75-ton ladles, from which it is then emptied into cupolas, to be, in turn, drawn off in small quantities and poured into waiting molds, is to behold an epic of industry—molten iron from the blast furnace's fierce flames poured into the mold itself, without the intervening pig-iron stage.

Going through the major plants of the industry is an experience one can never forget. Following the main processes in car fabrication, we pass from the foundry, where the fiery liquid is molded into parts, into the forge building, where they are heat-treated and shaped.

Here is a giant triphammer capable of delivering a four-ton blow, and yet so skillfully operated that it can be made to tap a watch without breaking the crystal, or to touch a finger ring so lightly as to leave only a slight grease mark thereon; there, a tremendously powerful press that shapes a crankshaft with the seeming ease with which a child presses out a mud pie.

Elsewhere we see a battery of pots, using, in heat-treating various parts that are to be subjected to hard wear and rough usage, enough molten cyanide every day to kill all the people in the Western Hemisphere (see page 64).

Leaving the forge department and passing on to the machine shop, one encounters a thousand mechanical marvels. There one sees immense multiple drill presses, some of them capable of boring more than fifty holes simultaneously in four directions, each perfectly true in its direction, in an engine block; piston-grinding machines that automatically grind four pistons at a single operation, facing the top and turning the outside diameter at the same time; screw machines that automatically feed themselves long steel rods, four or more at a time, and transform them into perfect screws—heads, threads, and slots.

A whole battery of machines in this department is busy milling the "cheeks" on the "throws" of crankshafts, each one doing what formerly required twelve different operations, on as many machines, each manned by an operator.

Another battery of machines is cutting teeth on gear-wheel blanks. One man attends a number of them, and all they ask is that he give them a regular supply of blanks and liberal streams of oil over the cutting surface.

FASHIONING FENDERS AND BRAKE DRUMS

Elsewhere an endless procession of engine blocks is coming down the line, each block being cut and trimmed into shape by powerful cutters to which iron seems little harder than cheese. One type of these milling machines takes a series of blocks and rotates them past the cutting tool instead of moving them one at a

GRINDING THE CYLINDERS OF A STANDARD "SIX" ENGINE

Each cylinder in a high-grade engine must be ground exactly true, both as to size and direction. It must not depart more than one ten-thousandth of an inch from standard size. Note the emery wheel in the fourth cylinder from the left. In a six-cylinder car, each piston makes 6,000 trips through its cylinder for every mile traveled (see text, pages 30-31).

A PRESS FOR MOLDING BAKELITE DISTRIBUTOR HEADS AND OTHER IGNITION PARTS

Bakelite is made by treating carbolic acid with formaldehyde, and comes to the automobile accessory manufacturer in a powdered form. He imbeds his terminals and other metal parts therein, and subjects it to high heat and heavy pressure, getting the fine, indestructible insulation required for his electrical parts, which do so much to reduce ignition difficulties.

A BIG ENGINE-BLOCK BORING MACHINE IN OPERATION

Boring some fifty holes, of various sizes and in four directions, at a single operation is typical of the methods of automobile manufacturers in reducing the cost of building cars by the elimination of unnecessary hand labor.

time back and forth on a platform. One of these machines takes the place of twelve of earlier design, occupies only a fifth as much floor space, and reduces the human factor to a minimum.

From the machine shop one passes to the stamp-press shop, where other wonders await him—machines that cut blanks out of sheet steel as easily as the housewife cuts cookies out of dough, and much faster; others that transform steel disks into brake drums at one operation; still others that stamp fenders out of sheet steel with a single movement.

Here are spot-welders that baste the two parts of an axle housing together just as a seamstress bastes a sleeve before sewing it. The operator holds the two pieces of steel together, touches a switch, melts a spot on the two edges, and causes the steel to run together. This binds the two parts together for the man who is to finish the job.

One watches cylinder-grinding, where $1/10,000$ of an inch is the limit of tolerance in departure from exact size; follows piston-ring inspection with measuring instruments, in which rays of light are made to reveal fine variances that escape detection by ordinary means; studies dynamometer tests that reveal the exact horsepower developed at all speeds; examines the machine that calculates the area of an irregular piece of leather a thousand times as fast as it could be determined by arithmetic! (see page 59).

Likewise, one is inclined to linger along the assembly lines, watching engines and transmissions and rear axles being built up and coming down to the main line where they meet the chassis and are made a part of it. The paint shop, where the enamel is sprayed on and the steel body is sent on moving platforms through the drying kilns; the upholstery and trimming

department—a score of fascinating activities beseech attention, but their "say" must be with pictures (see pages 11, 13, 16, 18, 53, 55-57, 59, 61, 62, and 64).

The employment of machinery in the making of automobiles and the quantity of product turned out are among the marvels of this mechanical age. If old-time hand methods were used, it is estimated that a single plant in the industry would require two million workmen where now less than 100,000 are employed, and even a "flivver" would cost almost as much as the most expensive car to-day.

A TRIBUTE TO GENIUS

The American tribute to the automotive engineer's genius has made his industry the third largest in the United States and has enabled it to bow petroleum into second place. The automotive vehicle manufacturer has become the largest producer of finished goods in the world.

Looking down the line of motor cars put out, from the Packards, Pierce Arrows, Lafayettes, Locomobiles, Lincolns, Cadillacs, and Marmons, with their superlative standards of construction; to the Fords, Stars, Grays, and Chevrolets, designed to meet the essential requirements of those of moderate means, we find that everywhere there is an amazing amount of mileage in them per dollar invested, when given proper care and operated at speeds consistent with their construction.

H. C. S.'s, Stutzes, Wintons, Hudsons, Studebakers, Chandlers, Nashes, Franklins, Buicks, Reos, Hupmobiles, Maxwells, Chalmers, Dodges, Durants, Overlands, and many others, offer a range of choice in price and type to meet every taste and every requirement, but

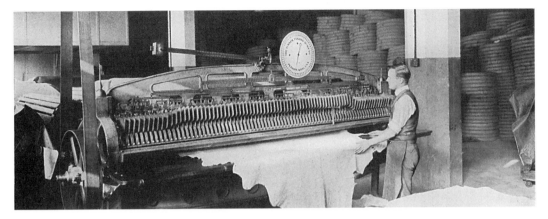

AN AUTOMATIC HIDE-MEASURING MACHINE

This mechanism is able to compute instantly the square footage of a hide with all its irregularities. As the hide passes through, every square inch is automatically noted and the total registered on the dial in front of the operator.

A MACHINE THAT FINISHES FOUR PISTONS
ON THE TOP AND SIDE WALLS SIMULTANEOUSLY

George Baldwin Selden, of Selden patent fame, probably lost untold millions by a simple little diary entry. His patent was applied for nearly two decades before the building of the first successful American automobile, but was not issued until years after. When he saw what is now the accepted type of four-cycle motor, he wrote, "Another of those d—d Dutch engines." On that entry the courts held he was not thinking of such an engine when he patented his vehicle, and therefore that the building of the modern motor car did not infringe his patent, although it was valid for other types of engines.

any one of them represents a good car within the price range to which it belongs.

It is true that the manufacturers, in the main, make big total profits, but these grow small when brought down to a per-car basis. Most of these profits arise, moreover, by economies. The Studebaker South Bend plant, for instance, spends $3,000,000 for a new foundry; this will pay for itself in the economies of a comparatively short time.

THE HIGH COST OF DISTRIBUTION

The high cost of distribution is one of the striking factors of the automotive industry. The economist who wrote that it costs as much to sell a car as to make it probably went a little beyond the mark, but at that, the margin between the wholesale and retail prices is vastly larger than that between cost of production and the wholesale price.

Economists generally agree that more than one-half the price the consumer pays for the commodities he uses represents the costs and profits of handling them between the producer and the consumer. The late President Harding called this one of the greatest problems of civilization, if indeed not the greatest.

The motor truck has been asked to help solve this problem, and it seems to be making a substantial contribution thereto. A big New York firm found that the ton-mile delivery cost fell from 48 cents with horses to 20 cents with motor trucks.

In Milwaukee, Wisconsin, the milk companies decided to motorize their quantity milk delivery, and the result was a saving of two cents a quart on their product.

A Detroit department store has instituted a new motorized delivery service and now delivers within a radius of 75 miles, giving a vast rural and small-town population a service never before thought possible.

A study of truck statistics shows that eighty-three out of every hundred built last year were of one-ton or less capacity. A quarter of a million trucks were built that year and there are now about a million in commission in the United States.

In most cases where the motor truck has gone into delivery service in competition with the horse, it has been able to cut down the delivery cost in almost as large a proportion as it accelerates the time of delivery. We all love the horse, but economy is the prime consideration of the business world.

The truck also has a vast field before it in handling the short-haul freight that the railroads now handle. Any rail shipment that is for less than forty miles is apt to be carried at a loss. The railroads, it is said, want to give this business to the motor truck. Likewise, they would gladly remove their freight depots from the centers of cities, since the interest on such investments wipes out the profits of package freight handling. They would like to have their freight stations outside of congested districts and let the motor trucks take care of the city delivery.

CINCINNATI RESULTS
SHOW WHAT TRUCKS CAN DO

In Cincinnati motorized freight terminals have been established. In a single year they released 66,000 cars for mainline movement on the railroads, eliminated 300,000 switching cuts, advanced freight movement over 52 hours, and cut the labor cost in half through the elimination of rehandling.

One of the abuses of the motor truck is to put it on long hauls that parallel railway lines. Statistics definitely show that long-haul truck

A STAMPING PRESS THAT COMPLETES FIVE FENDERS A MINUTE

This great machine turns out 2,700 fenders per day, one fender at each stroke. So accurate is the operation that the fender requires no further finishing touches, but is ready to be enameled as soon as the pressure of 225 tons is removed.

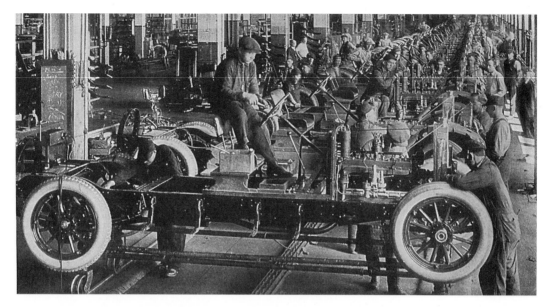

THE FINAL ASSEMBLY LINE IN A BIG AUTOMOBILE FACTORY

When cars were first built, all the parts were simply dumped in piles on the floor. Now a frame starts down one line, an engine block down another, a transmission and rear axle down others. When they all meet, they have each been assembled and are ready to be united into a completed chassis on the final assembly line.

FINISHING THE METAL WORK ON THE BODIES OF A QUALITY MAKE OF CAR

Such bodies as these require about a hundred days from raw material to finished product. The new steel, baked-enameled bodies go through the factory in less than two days (see text, page 37).

lines sooner or later go out of business, only to be succeeded by others which, in their turn, find the competition ruinous. But in the meantime, they have made uneconomic inroads into the earnings of the railroads and cut down the service rail lines can render to a fraction of its former efficiency.

One of the uneconomic situations which has developed in the past generation is strikingly illustrated between Dayton, Ohio, and Indianapolis, Indiana.

There used to be a good rail service between these two cities that yielded a reasonable profit to the railroads. Then there came into the field a new carrier—an interurban traction line. It so ate into the business of the railroads that they were forced to curtail their service.

But still later the fine motor highway between Dayton and Indianapolis was opened up, and it, in turn, made heavy inroads upon the traction line.

Some day there will be a coördination of our transportation facilities that will adjust such conditions, making each an asset rather than a liability to the other. When railroad, traction and motor lines are correlated properly, each will add to the strength of the others and the public will be vastly the gainer.

The truck is fast eliminating the horse from the cities of the country. Between 1910 and 1920 the number of horses in New York decreased from 128,000 to 56,000; in Chicago, from 68,000 to 30,000; in Philadelphia, from 50,000 to 19,000; in Baltimore from 15,000 to 7,000; in Cleveland, from 16,000 to 4,000.

The Quartermaster's Department of the Army, at Camp Holabird, under the direction of Arthur W. Herrington, is developing two types of trucks that promise to revolutionize truck construction for heavy duty. One of these types has a four-wheel drive, with over size pneumatic-tire equipment. This truck will go almost anywhere that caterpillar tractors can go, and some places that they cannot, in cross-country work and on wet clay roads; and on top of that, it will do anything that a regulation truck will do on good roads. As efficient as a caterpillar in bad going and as speedy as a regular truck on a good road surface, it can be built at a reasonable cost.

The other is a six-wheel truck capable of handling a 7½-ton load, with even less pressure per square inch of tire-road contact than the ordinary 3-ton solid-tire truck. The four rear wheels are assembled after the fashion of the ordinary railway-car truck, and are driven by a double differential from the propeller shaft.

Both of these trucks are built up out of standard parts, and not only will they develop new fields for automotive transportation in time of peace, but they will also constitute the types of heavy-duty vehicles the Army will want in the unhappy event America ever has to unsheathe its sword again.

THE TRACTOR'S PART
IN THE HORSELESS AGE

The farm naturally is the last stronghold of the horse. The natural inertia of the farmer has something to do with this. But more than that, the tractor that will serve him as well in its field as the motor car does in its sphere has not until now shown signs of appearing.

First of all, it must be a tractor that can utilize existing farm implements. An investment of $3,500,000,000 in horsedrawn equipment is too great to send to the scrap heap.

It must, therefore, be capable of operation by reins, just as if it were a team of horses. This gives freedom to the operator to attend the ma-

THE CYANIDE OF POTASSIUM FURNACES IN A DETROIT MOTOR-CAR PLANT

Heat-treating and case-hardening have done a vast deal toward making the automobile stand the strains to which every-day usage puts it. This one plant uses enough cyanide every day to destroy the entire population of the New World (see text, page 54).

ONE OF THE REASONS WHY PEOPLE OF MODERATE MEANS CAN AFFORD GOOD CARS

In the elimination of lost motion, automobile manufacturers are ever on the watch for improvements. In the machining of engine blocks older installations take one block at a time, put it on a bed and move the cutting tool back and forth over it, with each backward movement an idle one. The machine here takes a half dozen blocks and rotates them past the cutting tool, eliminating the idling back motion. Reduced cost of milling engine blocks is the result.

DRAGGING OUT STUMPS IS ONE OF THE MANY JOBS ASSIGNED THE TRACTOR
WHEN THE "BUSY SEASON" ON THE FARM IS PAST

chinery being pulled, as well as to the tractor itself.

In the second place, it must be so designed that it can be used in cultivating row crops like corn; it must be able to straddle one or two rows and turn in a small radius at the end.

In the third place, it must be able to render efficient belt-power service, so that the farmer can hitch it to a wood saw, a threshing machine, and whatnot.

The fourth requirement is that it shall take the place of the horses on the road as well as in the field, so that it may be fully able to substitute the horse.

Happily, all these specifications have been, or are being, filled except the last. To make a wheel that is readily converted from one with a cleat-studded rim for field duty into one with a smooth rim for road work is a task that is engaging the attention of the best engineers. One manufacturer says he will pay $25,000 for the wheel that completely meets this need.

A NEW ECONOMIC TRANSFORMATION

With Canada announcing a half-billion-bushels wheat crop, with Siberia on the eve of bonanza cereal farming, with Argentina and Australia developing in rapid strides, the

A REMINDER OF THE TIME
WHEN GRAIN WAS SOWN BROADCAST

Handpower gave way before horsepower a generation ago; and now, in its turn, horsepower is facing a formidable rival in tractor power.

American farmer must become a more efficient producer to meet their competition, which has much more to do with the present low prices of farm commodities than most people realize.

In those countries cheap lands produce large holdings and vast fields, where production costs per bushel can be driven down by highly organized power farming.

POWER FARMING AND PRODUCTION

Experience throughout the tractor farming belt shows that if the farmer values his labor at current rates, it costs less to sow and reap an acre of wheat with tractor-drawn equipment than with horse-drawn. Experiment-station records in our Western grain belt present striking illustrations of this. The reduction in labor costs goes down much faster than equipment and maintenance costs go up.

But that is only the beginning of the story. Power farming and horse cultivation of identical tracts in Kansas resulted in eleven years in the production of eight bushels of wheat on the power-farmed tract for every five on the horse-tilled land.

TRACTOR-SEEDING ON AN UP-TO-DATE FARM

Contrast this picture with the one above and note the progress a single generation has wrought.

The secret of this success of the tractor over the horse was that, with the former, the land could be plowed seven inches deep in July, while with the latter, owing to the heat in midsummer, it had to be plowed five inches deep in September.

As the July-plowed soil contains one and a half times as much moisture as the September-turned, and as deep plowing turns up more plant food than shallow, it is easy to account for the difference in yield.

These examples of lowered per-acre costs for cultivation through the elimination of high-priced labor, and increased per-acre yield through better methods of cultivation might be multiplied indefinitely.

THE DAWN OF A NEW ERA

We stand on the threshold of another transformation in farm life, as significant and as far-reaching as that which took place when the farmer laid away his scythe, grain cradle, and flail for the mower, the binder, and the threshing machine.

By substituting machines for hired hands, the farmer will lighten his heaviest load—high labor costs.

When the versatile utility tractors that are now ready to come on the market make their bows, the farmer will settle the labor question as he settled it with his binder and mower.

He will discover that he can so decrease his labor cost and increase his acre yield as practically to make two dollars grow where one grew before.

The substitution of power for horses will mean millions of people released from agriculture for industry, as was the case when the farmer substituted horses for men.

With more urban mouths to feed and backs to clothe, and fewer rural ones to provide for, a new day will dawn when the efficiency of the factory will come to the farm, and then the American farmer can do what the American automobile maker has done—meet the competition of the world and still make money.

And when the noontide of that day is reached, the great triumvirate—the passenger car, the freight truck, and the farm tractor—are destined to write a record of service to America that will stamp the automobile engineer as one of the foremost contributors to human welfare in all the history of mankind.

VOL. XLIII, No. 4   WASHINGTON   APRIL, 1923

AMERICA'S AMAZING RAILWAY TRAFFIC

By William Joseph Showalter

Author of "The Panama Canal," "How the World is Fed,"
"Industry's Greatest Asset—Steel," "Coal—Ally of American Industry," etc.,
in the National Geographic Magazine

IN THEIR rôle as arteries of commerce, the railroads of the United States carry the lifeblood of trade to the ends of the nation.

So great is that task that it is difficult to get an adequate picture of it; for the statistics of train-miles, car-miles, passenger-miles, and ton-miles expand into millions and billions so rapidly that only those who combine the industry of the busy bee and the patience of the suffering Job can reduce them to terms within the grasp of laymen.

If all the people of the United States were reviewed in single file, passing at the rate of one a second, forty months would elapse from the day the head of the column marched by to the hour the rear guard approached. Yet the annual transportation task devolving upon the railroads is equivalent to moving all these people, with eight tons of freight for each of them, from Paris, France, to Genoa, Italy.

Stated in another way, if Father Adam, according to Biblical chronology, had started a mixed train running down through the centuries, at a speed of 22 miles per hour, carrying 40 passengers and 346 tons of freight, and if that train had never stopped from then to now, it still would not have covered as great a distance or performed as large a passenger or freight service as the trains of the United States do in a normal year.

THE LENGTH OF AMERICA'S RAILWAYS

Counting all sidings, yards, and multiple tracks, there are approximately 375,000 miles of rails in the United States. How distant the first mile from the last will the better appear if it be told that the Twentieth Century Limited—the

"THE SPIRIT OF TRANSPORTATION"

Nothing that is material does more to make a nation great than its railroads. The interchange of raw products makes possible big industries; the free movement of commodities from producer to consumer makes available vast markets; opportunities are afforded for the flow of commerce and the intercourse of minds, thus welding the diverse sections of a wide-flung country into one mighty, homogeneous community. Above is a picture of some of the big engines of the Santa Fe in their Chicago station, seemingly endowed with life and impatient to be up and away on their journey to the shores of the Pacific.

crack New York Central flyer between New York and Chicago, maintaining an average terminal-to-terminal speed of approximately 50 miles per hour—would require from the birth of the New Year to within a fortnight of Thanksgiving to cover this mileage.

It is a far cry from the splendid four-track route, with grades reduced to negligible percentages, and curves all but eliminated, stretching between the major cities of the country, to the neglected single-track line, with grades everywhere and curves more numerous than tangents, stretching between Junctionville and Podunk, the latter characteristic of the railroads of 50 years ago and the former the latest development of the art of railroading.

Some two decades ago the freight traffic of the country had grown so heavy that curves and grades regarded as inconsiderable in the first half century of American railroading became serious obstructions to the free movement of traffic under 20th century conditions.

All over the United States one may today see traces of abandoned rights of way, meandering here and there in a fashion that makes the traveler think that the early engineers must have followed the cows about and plotted their paths, and remind him that tens of thousands of miles of railway had to be rebuilt to meet the nation's demands for better freight and passenger facilities.

MILLIONS FOR MINUTES

With the abandonment of these early railroads have come the splendid multiple-track highways, without which the present volume of traffic could not be handled.

A typical case of spending millions to save minutes and pennies appears in the history of the Lackawanna. That road was first built half a century ago, primarily as a coal-carrier between Scranton and New York. Money was not plentiful in those days; so many a compromise with grades and curves had to be made.

But a day dawned when the Lackawanna saw that if it were to compete with other companies it must have scores of the grades and curves on its line ironed out. Across New Jersey from Port Morris to Delaware Water Gap was a stretch of road, 39½ miles long, meandering about and dipping up and down as only old-fashioned roads did.

Nothing less than a cut-off would cure that situation, and so a line only three miles longer than air-line distance was laid out, shortening the route between Scranton and New York 11 miles.

Fills and cuts and tunnels required to carry the road diagonally across deep-valleyed watercourses and high-ridged watersheds made the cut-off one of the most expensive in the history of railway building; but it shortened the schedule of passenger trains by 20 minutes, cut down the running time of freight trains by an hour, and more than doubled the length of the average coal train moving over the Lackawanna; so that even a million dollars a mile spent to shorten the line proved one of the best investments that road ever made.

The same company did another spectacular thing in eliminating grades and curves when it built its famous viaduct across the Tunkhan-

DELAWARE RIVER BRIDGE AT SLATEFORD JUNCTION, PENNSYLVANIA

This is said to be the longest concrete bridge in the world. The track is carried 75 feet above high water and the piers go down to bed-rock, 61 feet below the ground. It forms a part of the Lackawanna cut-off in western New Jersey. The east end of the bridge is in New Jersey and the west end in Pennsylvania.

THE LUCIN CUT-OFF ACROSS THE GREAT SALT LAKE

He was a bold engineer who undertook to lay a railroad across Great Salt Lake. Urged on by an imperious executive, the engineer attempted the seemingly impossible. Sink-holes developed and structures that were months in building disappeared beneath the waves of the salt sea. But the faith of the executive never wavered. "We will pass!" was his motto, and to-day the thousands who ride over that cut-off give no thought to the battle staged there between man and Nature (see text, page 72).

nock Valley. That viaduct is nearly half a mile long, and as high as a 20-story building. The cut-off of which it is a part saves 3.6 miles between Scranton and Binghamton, but even though built at a cost of three and a third million dollars per mile, the Lackawanna made a fine investment in its construction (see illustration, page 77).

A HIGH-GRADE LOW-GRADE RAILWAY

The Pennsylvania main line between Philadelphia and Pittsburgh strikes the lay traveler as being about the last word in grade and curve reduction; and, so far as passenger trains go, it is. But such a tremendous freight traffic as the Pennsylvania handles eastward called for even better grades than the main line offers. The traffic from the East to the West is so much lighter than that moving from the West to the East that the engineers can concede much to westward grades.

So it was decided to build a low-grade freight line from Pittsburgh to New York. That line now is in operation, except for 23 miles over the Allegheny Mountains, where the grade is 52.8 feet to the mile. Its steepest grade in the

FIVE MODERN MEANS OF AMERICAN TRANSPORTATION

The rivers of the country carry a considerable tonnage; coal moves down the Ohio and the Mississippi from Pittsburgh to New Orleans at a fraction of the rail cost. The electric lines of the country, urban and interurban, carry some ten billion passengers annually. Over the improved highways of the United States, motor cars cover billions of miles. The canals were our first important freight arteries, and as traffic problems increase are expected to come into their own again. The railways, as the years come and go, will probably be forced to relinquish low-class freight to the canals and find themselves kept busy handling high-class commodities.

path of eastbound traffic is only 17 feet to the mile, up which an engine can pull any train that it is able to start on the level. The Pennsylvania has for some time been studying the question of electrifying this heavy grade over the Allegheny Mountains, which includes the famous "Horseshoe Curve."

THE LUCIN CUT-OFF

When the Union Pacific was building its line toward the Golden Gate, the Great Salt Lake lay across its path. In those days it did what

any other railroad would have done—it made a detour.

That detour became a nightmare to the management several decades later, for it added 44 miles to the journey from Omaha to San Francisco, made every train lift itself an unnecessary 1,500 feet, and forced all trains to follow needless curves equivalent to 10 full circles.

So the Lucin Cut-Off across the Great Salt Lake, costing $10,000,000, was built. It proved a good investment, for the curves, climbs, and distance eliminated saved some two hours of

HELL GATE BRIDGE, GIVING A THROUGH RAIL CONNECTION
BETWEEN NEW ENGLAND AND THE SOUTH

Built in the form of a great crescent, Hell Gate Bridge, spanning East River and making possible the through expresses between Boston and Washington, is one of the world's finest examples of bridge engineering. With the Connecting Railway, of which it is a part, it required four years to build, at a cost of $27,000,000. In the foreground is the 1,000-foot steel span, the largest in the world, containing four times as much steel as the Woolworth Building. In the lower right-hand corner is a bit of Long Island. Beyond the steel span is Ward's Island, and above that Randall's Island. The channel in the background is Harlem River, and beyond that the southern edge of the Bronx.

precious time and millions of dollars in operating expenses.

The Canadian Pacific, which gets a little look-in on the United States by crossing the State of Maine, has been one of the roads to modernize its pioneer lines in many places, particularly in the Rockies and the Selkirks. In the region of Kicking Horse River in the Rockies there was a heavy grade more than four miles long, with a rise of 237.6 feet to the mile. It was known as the Big Hill. Getting a train up that hill was a tremendous task, four to six engines being required. But getting it down was an even more arduous undertaking.

Switches were introduced along the line, and those who operated them had strict instructions to listen for a certain whistle signal. It meant that the train giving it had gotten out of

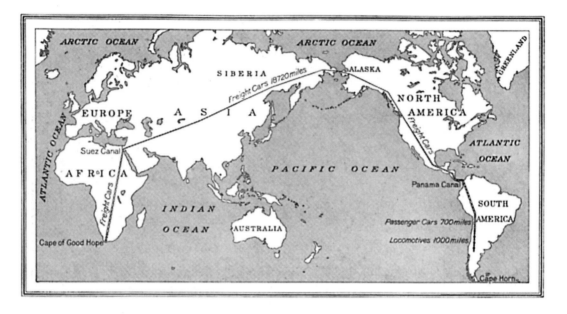

A GRAPHIC REPRESENTATION OF THE VASTNESS
OF THE ROLLING STOCK EQUIPMENT OF AMERICA'S RAILROADS

If all the freight-service cars, all of the passenger-service cars, and all of the locomotives in the United States were coupled together, they would make a train reaching from the Cape of Good Hope, via the Isthmus of Suez, Bering Strait, and the Panama Canal, nearly to Cape Horn (see text).

control and must be shunted off onto the siding which ran up a grade, thus effecting a stop.

CANADIAN PACIFIC
BUILDS SPIRAL TUNNELS

To overcome these difficulties, the Canadian Pacific decided to build two spiral tunnels, the first of their kind in America.

The first of these "corkscrew" bores is 3,200 feet long under Cathedral Mountain. A train entering from the east turns in the direction whence it came, and, after emerging, crosses Kicking Horse River. Then it enters the second spiral tunnel, and, after descending an elliptical curve, emerges, headed west again.

The road in this relocation doubles back on itself twice, spirals its way under two mountains, and crosses the river twice in order to avoid the Big Hill. The improvement cost $1,500,000, but two engines do the work of five or six, and a 10-mile speed has become a 25-mile gait.

The Grand Trunk, in order to command its share in the through business from Chicago to the East, had to find a way to eliminate the river difficulty at Detroit. The St. Clair River connecting Lakes Huron and Ontario is here about a half-mile wide. Bridging it was out of the question. Car ferries were too slow. Hence the railway officials decided to tunnel under the

PASSENGERS ABOARD THE GREAT NORTHERN'S FAMOUS ORIENTAL LIMITED
ENJOYING THE SCENERY IN THE SKYKOMISH COUNTRY, WASHINGTON

THE RAILROAD BRIDGE ABOVE THE NIAGARA RAPIDS

Once this bridge was regarded as a wonder. To-day it is being proposed to bridge the Hudson with a huge suspension structure the cables of which will be 60 inches in diameter as compared with the 15-inch cables of the Brooklyn Bridge. The main span will be three times as long as that of Hell Gate Bridge (see page 73) and its total length more than a mile and a half. Another huge terminal station, to accommodate those roads which do not enter either of the two existing New York terminals, is a part of the tentative project.

river. They ran steam engines through, but this soon proved so unsatisfactory that a substitute had to be found. The B. & O. pioneering in Baltimore showed the feasibility of electricity, and so the St Clair Tunnel was electrified, with such success that under-river electrified tunnels became a matter of recognized engineering practice.

Most roads to-day are old ones transformed by extensions and relocations, but once in a

while a new line is built without any of the limitations imposed by former conditions.

Such a railway is the Virginian, extending from Deepwater, West Virginia (near Charleston) to Sewalls Point, Virginia (near Norfolk)—a coal road pure and simple. "I want a road from the West Virginia coal fields to the sea," said H. H. Rogers. "It must be a road on which a modern locomotive can haul 80 fifty-ton carloads of coal from the mines to the sea-

THE VIADUCT ACROSS THE TUNKHANNOCK, IN PENNSYLVANIA

The apparent slenderness of the piers of this bridge is due to their great height. The men standing under the foreground arch give some idea of the viaduct's vast proportions (see text, page 71).

board without breaking up the train. The grades eastbound must not exceed 10 feet to the mile."

It was a large order, but one which the engineer daringly executed, the only exception being a stretch of 11 miles, where the eastbound grade is over a 100 feet to the mile.

But here the largest locomotives in the world act as pushers and raise the 80-car train intact over the crest of the line. A whole new coal territory has been tapped, and if the Virginian Railway hauls 10,000,000 tons of the mined product to market annually it can oper-

ONE OF THE LOCOMOTIVES OF THE VIRGINIAN RAILWAY (SEE TEXT, PAGE 76)

The "largest locomotive in the world" never maintains its prestige long. Nearly every year sees a larger one built. The Virginian's latest compound articulated Mallets, with their twenty drivers, 449 tons weight, and 147,200 pounds tractive effort, are now the giants of the rails. They can comfortably handle seventy-five 120-ton cars from the mines to the seashore, with the help of a pusher up the mountain grade, and have done much better than that in demonstration tests. On the heavy grades they burn coal at a rate of six tons an hour.

ate for 400 years before exhausting its freight supply.

A VAST NUMBER OF ENGINES AND CARS

When one comes to the rolling stock of all the railroads of the United States, consisting as it does of 2,348,000 freight cars, 65,000 locomotives, and 53,000 passenger-train cars, and attempts to visualize its immensity, perhaps the best picture to be obtained will come from imagining all these engines and cars coupled into one train.

Suppose this train to be on a sort of vast horseshoe curve, sweeping through Africa, Asia, North America, and South America via the Suez Canal, Siberia, Alaska, and Panama (see map).

So long will the train be that when the last caboose is at the Cape of Good Hope the forward engine will be only 1,200 miles out of Cape Horn.

BRIDGING A CANYON IN ARIZONA

beyond Antofagasta, Chile, and the engines would still further extend the train's length, so that it would reach nearly to Valdivia, Chile—a train, indeed, stretching from 30 degrees south latitude in Africa to the Arctic Circle in Asia, and back to 40 degrees south latitude in South America!

What a vast series of contrasts among the thousand miles of locomotives in service on the railroads of the United States! Here is one that made its appearance in the days of brass bands around the boiler, red stripes and stars around the smokestack, and a name on the cab. Here is the old 999, that once hauled the Empire State Express on its road to fame, and later took the prosaic job of hauling light freights on a branch line. Down the track is a big Mallet articulated engine weighing 449 tons, having a length of 105 feet, and possessing cylinders of a diameter equal to that of the boilers of many locomotives built since the Civil War.

The conductor on the rear platform might listen to the break of the waves on the South African coast while the brakeman on the forward freight car gave ear to the ripple of the waves on the shore of Lake Titicaca, Peru.

The passenger-train cars would add enough length to the train to make it reach 100 miles

A FREIGHT LOCOMOTIVE'S STORY

The work of an average freight locomotive is no light chore. Its job is to haul a 1,300-ton train 56½ miles each day, a traffic task

PIERCING THE ROCKS

The Rocky Mountains and the Sierra Nevada are formidable barriers to
a great commerce; but with tunnel and bridge, trestle and cut, mountains have been removed, and the citrus fruits of California and the fine
timbers of Oregon and Washington are exchanged across these erst-
while isolating barriers for a thousand products of the East.

sharp curves, takes a heavy
toll out of the freight engine's
frame, with the result that for
a full quarter of its time it is
on the operating table in the
engine hospital, or waiting its
turn to go there.

When the big mogul's
performance is measured by
the energy it is able to ex-
tract from a pound of coal, it
looks like a sheer waster of
fuel, for only about one-
twentieth of that energy is
transformed into drawbar
pull. But when one remem-
bers that, for all its limitations, the average freight engine is able to move 10 tons
of train a full mile for each
cent's worth of coal burned,
its record does not seem a
bad one.

THE ELECTRIC
ENGINE'S DEFIANCE

The electric locomotive,
of which there are several
hundred in operation in the
United States, could tell a
startling story.

It was born of necessity.
When the B. & O. wanted to
burrow under Baltimore,
coal-burning locomotives
seemed out of the question

equivalent to moving 20 tons from the Statue
of Liberty to the Golden Gate.

Hauling such a train, rain or shine, in warm
weather or in cold, over heavy grades and around

for a tunnel so long. So an electric substitute
was created. It showed such good results that
one railroad after another tried electrified tunnels, uniformly with success.

Finally the Pennsylvania and the New York Central decided that the electric's past performances had been good enough to justify their building vast terminals in New York City into which no steam locomotive could be admitted. The electric engine's cleanness made possible under-the-river tunnels in the case of the Pennsylvania, and a two-level track-layout in the case of the New York Central.

Electrifying the terminals led to electrified approaches, and wherever electricity got a chance to compete with steam, the former never lost the argument. The electrically propelled train could show the steam train its green flags at the rear any day, and its red lights any night. The electric engine was able to get a 1,000-ton train started from a standstill more quickly than the steam locomotive, at every trial of their relative power.

In the matter of cleanness and economy of operation, also, every test showed in electricity's favor. So the Pennsylvania, New York Central, and the New Haven began to electrify their suburban lines.

Seeing the striking results of electrification around New York, the Chicago, Milwaukee & St. Paul Railway Co. decided to give the electric engine a tryout on a long stretch of its transcontinental line. It first electrified a division extending from Harlowton, Montana, to Avery, Idaho (near St. Maries), a distance of 440 miles. This section of the C., M. & St. P. crosses the three ridges constituting the Rocky Mountains, and at one place climbs to 6,300 feet.

When put to work hauling trains over that section, the electric locomotives began to show their real mettle. Terminal performances, commuter-zone competitions, and tunnel electrifications are all well enough, but when one comes down to essentials, a long stretch of road with three mountains to cross, innumerable grades to negotiate, and all kinds of weather to face—there is the place to put a locomotive to the real test.

Their performance astonished even electricity's chief supporters. The railroad company found it could operate its trains much more efficiently with 42 electrics than with 112 steam-engines. With the former type it was able to increase the length of each train by a fifth, thereby reducing the number of trains required. Likewise, the running time was cut down by a fifth. The electrics, in fact, demonstrated that they could increase the capacity of a single-track railroad to a point approaching double-track capacity under steam operation.

Many a time a train hauled by a "double header" of steam locomotives rolled up to the electrified division two hours late, after a bitter struggle with the elements. Radiation from their boilers weakened them, and snow slowed down their pace.

But the electrics are never happier than when there is zero weather around, and they made up all the time the steam-engines lost.

REGENERATIVE BRAKES AT WORK

Not only did the big motors demonstrate their power to pull trains up 2 per cent grades that would break a steam locomotive's heart, and at a speed that even three of the latter could not maintain, but when they got to the top of the mountain they taught a new lesson—superior efficiency in climbing down again.

Being equipped with what are known as "regenerative" brakes, the electric's motor, by the throwing of a switch, is transformed into a dynamo, and the surplus momentum of the train rolling down the mountain is expended

A SECTION OF A 16,000-TON COAL TRAIN HAULED OVER THE VIRGINIAN RAILWAY

When the Virginian Railway was built, it was planned to run trains of eighty 50-ton cars from the mines to deep water. In 1909 traffic demands called for eighty-five 50-ton cars. In 1914 it was found necessary to add another five cars to the train. Later it was decided to build 120-ton cars, which would make it possible for a single-track line to do what a double-track line could do with the lighter equipment. Brakes were devised and engines built, making possible the handling of a 16,000-ton train over the line with one locomotive, except in the mountains, where a pusher is added. Such a train was handled in 1921, and this picture shows, at the extreme left, some of the 100 loaded cars used in the demonstration. After passing the Blue Ridge, 10 additional cars were added, making a 17,500-ton train, the heaviest ever hauled in the history of railroading.

in driving this dynamo and sending the electricity thus generated back into the transmission line.

The problem of getting a steam-drawn train down from the crest of the Rockies was frequently as serious as that of dragging it up. The airbrakes frequently were hard to manage, the wheels often got red hot, the shoes sometimes melted.

But with "regenerative" braking, things have changed. All the momentum the brakes had to absorb and waste goes back into the transmission line, to be used as power to pull some other train up the mountain.

When a steam locomotive has its fires banked in the roundhouse it burns 200 pounds of coal an hour; when getting up steam it requires 800 pounds; when standing on side track

AN ELECTRIFIED ROAD IN THE CASCADES

With its Cascade and Rocky Mountain divisions electrified, the Chicago, Milwaukee and St. Paul Railway has taught America how to conserve its fuel supplies. Rivers running down the mountains pull heavy trains up, and a trip by rail without coal-gas and cinders, and minus jerks and jars, becomes a delightful excursion amid some of the world's most majestic landscapes. The overhead wire type of transmission (shown above) is used on the Milwaukee, the New Haven, and the Pennsylvania main line out of Philadelphia. The Pennsylvania Terminal and the New York Central use the third rail for power transmission.

or at stations it burns 500 pounds, and when coasting downhill 1,000 pounds.

In none of these situations do electrics require any power at all. Coasting down the mountain side, they can pay back from a fourth to a half as much as they borrowed to climb the mountain.

Without a jerk, without noise, without smoke, and without a cinder, they take their trains up the mountains and down again, at 20 miles an hour on even so heavy a grade as a rise

of 105 feet to the mile, and at 60 miles on the straightaway level.

THE LONGEST ELECTRIC ROAD IN THE WORLD

So gratifying was the electrification of the Harlowton-Avery branch to the Chicago, Milwaukee & St. Paul authorities that they decided to electrify the line from Seattle to Othello. This leaves only a 200-mile stretch to be electrified between the eastern approach to the Rockies and the Pacific Ocean, and gives the United States the longest electrified railroad in the world.

But the test of which the electric locomotive may be proudest took place not so long ago at Erie, Pennsylvania. One of them, just out of the shops on the St. Paul's new order, was pitted against two of the steam giants of the New York Central. They could not be matched in a tug of war, for, pulling against one another, a drawbar would be sure to pull out, with perhaps dangerous results.

So a pushing contest was staged instead. The two big steam locomotives were coupled together, and thus entered the fray. On a long stretch of track their engineers were told to open the throttles wide. With current off, the electric rival was no obstacle in their path, and they were soon taking it down the track at a passenger-train pace.

Then something happened; the engineer in the electric slowly turned on the current. The speed of the big locomotives began to slacken, and their smokestacks started to spout black smoke in a way that told how hard they were laboring.

Slower and slower they moved; harder and harder they worked, as though they were dragging a tremendous train up a heart-breaking grade; but with all that they could do they continued to lose speed.

Finally, though their throttles were still wide open and their cylinders were hissing with the pent-up steam that was unable to drive the big moguls forward, they were forced to a dead standstill.

But the pause was only for an instant. Still pushing with the last ounce of energy within them, their grip on the rails gave way and they bowed to their master—the electric locomotive. The latter not only had stalled them, but, turning on them, was driving them back in full retreat, in spite of the fact that they continued to strain every rod in their effort to check their onrushing rival.

But, even with that sturdy proof of its supremacy, the electric was not content. Again it allowed itself to be pushed down the track by its two big contestants. Again, with wide-open throttles they rushed it along at high speed. But again a little switch on the electric engine was thrown, a little switch which converted the motor that had overpowered its antagonists into a dynamo that acted as a brake.

Again the big giants began to labor, to shiver at the load they were encountering, to slow down under the burden. Slower and slower they moved, harder and harder they labored, but in vain! For, whether plunging forward, motor-driven, or holding back, regenerative-braked, the electric showed itself their master and proved itself the Samson of rail transportation.

The argument was over, and since that day railroad men everywhere have realized that the electric locomotive is destined eventually to succeed the steam locomotive wherever traffic is heavy and trains frequent.

Already roads are planning in that direction. The Pennsylvania, the Virginian, and many other lines are reckoning with electrification of busier divisions as an end to be aimed at.

WHAT UNIVERSAL ELECTRIFICATION WOULD SAVE

How much the electrification of the railroads of the country will save is strikingly shown by an investigation based on the St. Paul's experience and other data. This shows that electricity can be produced at 2½ pounds of coal per kilowatt hour, and that 53,000,000 tons would

TANK CARS AT A LOADING STATION: EAST CHICAGO, INDIANA

Although a large percentage of our oil moves by pipe line, the railroads annually handle more than 1,000,000 carloads of refined petroleum and nearly 200,000 carloads of the crude product. The petroleum train required to move a year's product would be, with its motive power, more than 10,000 miles long.

suffice to produce all the electricity required to move the freight of the United States—a saving of more than 100,000,000 tons a year.

These figures do not deduct anything for the added saving made possible by the use of hydroelectric power—the white coal of the country's unharnessed rivers. They are based on all power being produced by coal-driven dynamos.

Think of five big carloads of coal being wasted every single minute of the year; of five Niagaras running unharnessed to the sea! There you have a measure of what the electric locomotive promises to save, once it supplants the steam locomotive as the source of rail transportation's power.

With all their lines electrified there would be no reason for the railroads hauling a ton of coal for themselves. There are hundreds of power sites that could be developed, which would greatly reduce the coal tonnage required to drive the dynamos necessary to generate sufficient current to move all the trains of the country.

The power remaining to be supplied by coal could be generated at the mouth of the mine and sent out over wires.

To be relieved of the transportation of approximately 150,000,000 tons of coal a year would mean the saving of more than 3,000,000 carloads of freight, or 60,000 trainloads of 50 cars each. In other words, the coal trains required to haul the fuel used by the railroads themselves to-day would fill eight tracks reaching from Sandy Hook to Golden Gate, and all of this tremendous train movement would be saved by electrification of all lines.

The saving effected if electrification were adopted only on the Atlantic seaboard from Boston to Washington is strikingly shown in a report prepared, at the instance of former Secretary of the Interior, Franklin K. Lane, by the United States Geological Survey, under the direction of Dr. George Otis Smith.

This report, entitled "A Superpower System for the Region between Boston and Washington," shows that in 1930 the territory in question, for its municipal, industrial, private, and railroad purposes, will require 31 billion kilowatt hours of power, which could be furnished under a coordinated power system at a saving of $239,000,000 per annum.

In the case of the railroads, 19,000 out of 36,000 miles of track could be profitably electrified, at an annual saving in operating costs of $81,000,000, on a capital investment of $570,000,000.

To-day the average steam locomotive works eight hours a day, while the average electric is ready for twenty hours a day service.

It is estimated that there will be a doubling of traffic in this zone by 1930, and that the cost of electrification would be less than the cost of added facilities necessary in adhering to steam power.

One of the secrets of the electric engine's efficiency as compared with the steam locomotive is the greater adhesion of its drivers to the rails. Indeed, it can run twice as fast at maximum adhesion as the steam locomotive.

Some roads are beginning to use motor buses with marked success for the transportation of passengers on lines where the traffic is light. The Pennsylvania's western lines, feeling the pinch of competition from interurban electric lines and highway bus lines, are turning to motorized train service in order to reduce the cost of operation to a point in keeping with the revenues derived.

THE FREIGHT CAR'S SHARE IN THE WORLD'S WORK

When one sees a string of freight cars, some of them for carrying live stock, others for moving products needing refrigeration or ventilation, still others for hauling such diverse

WHEN A LOCOMOTIVE GOES TO THE HOSPITAL

Pulling trains day after day takes a heavy toll out of the engines. More than a fourth of the locomotives in the freight service are always either in the "engine hospital" or awaiting their turn to go there. The average engine burns 243 pounds of coal for every mile it runs.

LOADING A PASSENGER CAR AT SEATTLE FOR SHIPMENT TO ALASKA

Alaska as a tourist resort is one of the certain developments of the future. The railways already built there, including the Government line, bring one to the front door of some of America's finest scenery in this immensely important part of Uncle Sam's domain.

products as coal and oil, bulk molasses and ore, it is probably with little realization of the stories they might tell.

If their several stories were made into one composite tale, we would learn that the average car in a recent year ran about 22 miles a day, carried 27.8 tons of freight per load, and secured about 17 loads during the year. One-third of the 9,200 miles it traveled was as an empty.

One does not have to study transportation problems long to find out what a valued public servant the little-appreciated and unpretentious freight car actually is. There is one of them for every eight families in the country, and to them agricultural and industrial America owes a tremendous debt.

What would bonanza crops be worth if there were no freight cars to carry them to the markets of the nation and to start them to the hungry mouths of the world?

How could great factories thrive without the raw materials and the fuel the freight car brings to them, or without the many markets to which it gives them access?

"You never miss the water till the well runs dry" might be paraphrased into "You never ap-

A BIG ENGINE OF THE MICHIGAN CENTRAL

A locomotive's efficiency is largely determined by the proportion of its weight which it can put on the drivers. With such heavy trains as modern traffic requires, an engine must have a powerful grip on the rails.

THE DE WITT CLINTON RUNS ONCE MORE

This ancient and honorable train recently left its comfortable "siding" in the great hall of the Grand Central Station and took to the rails, under its own steam, for a little airing below Riverside Drive. It made eight miles an hour between 96th and 116th streets. Later it was loaded on cars and taken to Chicago. When railroads were first built it was solemnly decided by the London Philosophical Society that trains could never be permitted to run more than twelve miles an hour, since a greater speed would drive crazy all the people who chanced to live in the neighborhood of the right of way.

preciate the freight car till there's a car shortage." Indeed, the freight cars are the red corpuscles of the body politic, through which the oxygen of industry and the nutriment of commerce reach the cells that constitute our national life.

In order to obviate the building of large numbers of new freight cars, a national campaign has been started to increase their average daily mileage, to add to their average load, and to cut down the number of days they

are out of service awaiting and undergoing repairs.

The railroad executives responsible for the campaign want to speed up the cars, so that they will average 30 miles a day instead of the 23 they have been making. They want to increase the average load by 2.2 tons, and to cut down the average daily number on the "sick list" from 7 per cent to 4 per cent.

This would appear to the layman a very easy task. Yet the railroad man realizes that it is vastly more difficult than it seems. The fact is that thirteen-fourteenths of a car's year is spent off of the main tracks, either being switched around some yard, being loaded or unloaded, undergoing repairs, or just standing idly by waiting for something to turn up.

HOW A FREIGHT CAR SPENDS ITS TIME

Of its year the average car spends fourteen weeks on loading and unloading tracks; six weeks being switched into and out of trains and onto and off of loading tracks; two weeks awaiting shippers' orders; five weeks working its way through the maze of division yards; nine weeks in delivery from one road to another.

Then there are three weeks more lost by its arrival at its destination on Sundays and holidays, and five more while going through the repair shops. Slack seasons cause it another two weeks of idleness.

These items show forty-six weeks out of the year spent off of the road. Of the remaining forty-three days, which represent its gross time on the road, eleven may be counted off for time spent running empty in search of a load, and five

more may be deducted for delays incident to washouts, congestion, and the like.

All of which so taxes the car's time that it is able to spend only 27 days of actual running under load, and all of which tends to make an average of 30 miles per day a hard one to attain.

Thirty tons per car, the second aim of the railroads to-day, is almost as difficult of realization as 30 miles per day. Even under the severest stress of the war period, when every shipper made it a point of patriotism to get his cars loaded to capacity, it wasn't possible to reach that standard of loading efficiency.

In the first place, a stock car carries less than 10 tons of hogs, less than 11 of sheep and goats, and less than 12 of horses and mules. Likewise, box cars load less than 13 tons of hay and straw, cotton, wool, and eggs. On the other hand, coal cars force the average loading upward. During the second quarter of 1920 they moved more than 50 tons of bituminous coal, nearly 48 tons of anthracite, and more than 51 tons of iron ore.

The third aim of the railway managers is to shorten the time lost by the cars forced out

THE LARGEST "IRON HORSE" IN THE WORLD

This tremendous steed of the rails is the one that hauled a 17,500-ton train across south-side Virginia (see page 82), thus setting a world's record that will probably hold good longer than most railroad records do. It was built at the American Locomotive Works.

of service by bad condition. It is estimated that by a little careful scheming the average car's "sick leave" can be cut down to 14 days a year.

If the slogan of "30 miles per day, 30 tons per load, and 14 days for 'sick leave'" could be transformed into an achievement, the railroads would have additional service out of its cars already in commission equal to that which could be rendered by 260,000 new ones. An additional mile per day would equal the mileage of 100,000 new ones; an additional ton per day would give as much service as 80,000 new cars could render, and the reduction of "sick leave" to 14 days would yield the same results as the addition of 80,000 new cars.

"TRAMP STEAMERS" OF THE RAILS

Freight cars have a way of wandering from their own lines and becoming the rail counterparts of tramp steamers. When the demand for

A CAR DUMP IN A BALTIMORE FREIGHT TERMINAL

The old-fashioned method of shoveling grain out of cars is getting too slow for these modern days of heavy freight traffic, and the grain dump has come to keep company with the coal dump. A whole carload can be sent to the bins in a jiffy.

cars is acute, it is very much cheaper for a railroad to keep a "foreign" car than to return it to its home line; for the "per diem" charge for a foreign car is only one dollar a day.

Not long after the outbreak of the World War a St. Louis car-builder had an order for some freight cars from a California road. He started one west loaded, to save haulage charges. It delivered its load and then began to wander around. It made two or three trips to the Atlantic seaboard, a half dozen up and down the country, and finally, long after the armistice, reached its destination. There are instances of cars wandering around the country for seven years before setting wheels on home rails once more.

The freight car is the Cinderella of the transportation household. The passenger car flits about at high speed, day after day, and never would be able to support itself except for the toiling of its humble sister. If the passenger trains had to pay their half of all the expenses of railroad operation—for they make half the train mileage—they would show one of those dreaded red-ink balances in the profit-and-loss account.

The average passenger car runs far enough to make two trips around the earth every year, and some of them run for a full generation—first, usually, in the big express trains, then on the mainline locals, and finally out on some "jerk-water" branch or in the dollar-excursion equipment.

HAULING THE NATION'S FREIGHT

Turning from tracks and rolling stock to freight, one finds an equally startling story of the amazing proportions of railroad transportation.

The national balance sheet of work accomplished in 1919, which year is taken as the most nearly normal of any since the armistice, showed that 1,096,000,000 tons of freight were loaded into cars, and that the average ton was hauled 301 miles.

That represents the loading of a pile of merchandise as big as the great Pyramid of Cheops and hauling it from Washington, D. C., to New Haven, Connecticut, every eighteen hours.

If we could load the tremendous store of freight that moves in a year's time into one string of cars, it would be 312,000 miles long.

Imagine, if you can, a huge transcontinental railroad yard, stretching from New York to Seattle, via the meanderings of the Pennsylvania and the St. Paul, through Pittsburgh, Chicago, Milwaukee, St. Paul, Butte, and Spokane; and then imagine one hundred tracks in this vast continent-spanning yard packed solid with cars—box cars, coal cars, tank cars, refrigerator cars, stock cars, and flat cars—each and every one of them filled with the products of a nation's industry! That will give you a picture of the vastness of the interchange of commodities between the communities of a busy nation.

Forty of these tracks would be filled with the products of the nation's mines, 29 with the merchandise of its factories, 18 with the commodities that come from its farms, and 11 with forest products.

ITEMS OF OUR ANNUAL WAY BILL

If one wishes an itemization of some of the individual commodities included in those major groups, it may best be given in terms of trains standing in this imaginary transcontinental yard, with cabooses resting on the banks of the Hudson.

The butter and cheese moving by freight (there are no statistics of commodities moving by express) would fill a train reaching almost to Huntingdon, Pennsylvania.

The American hen gives the railroads more traffic as a producer of eggs than the American cow contributes through her output of butter and cheese, for the egg train would exceed by more than a hundred miles the length of the one carrying butter and cheese, and would reach considerably beyond Johnstown. There are no comprehensive statistics which would enable one to estimate the length of the annual milk and cream train, as these products are hauled largely by express.

Our love of "something to drink" brings to the railroads more traffic than our demands for something to wear, the textiles requiring some three thousand fewer cars than beverages, which would load a train reaching from Hoboken, New Jersey, to Alliance, Ohio.

The annual freight traffic in horses and mules, despite the competition of the automobile, sends some 80,000 carloads over the rails—

A "CONTAINER CAR" OPERATING BETWEEN NEW YORK AND CHICAGO

A new departure for "L. C. L." (less than carload) shipments is the burglar-proof container car, consisting of several sections, each of which is loaded by the shipper, at his plant, and hauled to the freight yard by truck. Here the several sections are put on a specially designed flat car and shipped to their destination, where they are transferred to other trucks and delivered unopened to the consignee. This saves numerous handlings and many damage claims.

AN AIRPLANE VIEW OF THE CLEARING EAST CLASSIFICATION YARD, NEAR CHICAGO

This picture shows the layout of a modern classification yard. Two trains to be "broken up" and their cars made up into other trains may be seen in the foreground. The "hump" (see text, page 98) is on the near side of the little house spanning the tracks in the foreground, and the slope runs down into the yard. Up in this bridge house are men who operate electrically controlled switches. They press a given button, the corresponding switch is set, and the cars intended for the train being made up on the track which this switch opens are uncoupled and allowed to roll by gravity to their appointed position. Clearing Yard, as a whole, is five miles long, contains 180 miles of track and 599 switches, and can handle 10,000 cars a day.

enough to make up a train reaching to a point considerably beyond Bucyrus, Ohio—while the train required to represent our citrus-fruit movement would stretch from Hoboken, New Jersey, to Lima, Ohio.

American devotion to "my lady Nicotine" contributes considerably to the traffic task of the railroads. In a recent year more than 90,000 carloads of tobacco and tobacco products moved by freight, and the train required to move it

would be some 750 miles long—extending all the way to Fort Wayne, Indiana.

That we are considerably addicted to the use of canned foods is shown by the fact that those moving by freight in a recent year would fill a train reaching from the banks of the Hudson almost to the banks of the Wisconsin.

The American sweet tooth, likewise, is well catered to by the railroads. Sugar, syrup, glucose, and molasses moving by freight during a

A ROTARY SNOW PLOW IN OPERATION

The railroads have their hardest struggles when the heavy snows begin to fall. In the Pacific Coast mountains, snow 20 feet deep on the level is not unusual. Only the big rotaries, driven by one or two big engines, will suffice to pierce the big drifts that so frequently occur. Sometimes it takes 60 minutes, even with these giant machines, to go 60 feet in attacking such drifts.

single year yield nearly 200,000 carloads of traffic—enough to make up a train whose headlight would illuminate the banks of the Missouri River at Mobridge, South Dakota, while its caboose was still in the Jersey City yards.

Even at that, the humble potato can go our sweet goods one better, requiring nearly 25,000 more cars. Our annual potato train is more than 1,800 miles long and would reach to a point within 100 miles of the Montana border.

The American hen, in addition to her egg contribution to the freight traffic of the country, makes a second large contribution; the train required to move the poultry she offers would fill a track reaching from the banks of the Hudson to the foothills of the Rockies.

The ice moving by rail as freight is a very small percentage of that used by the American people, and yet the cars required for its movement would fill a track reaching well into the valley of the Yellowstone, while the cotton train's forward engine would be farther west than the western boundary of Yellowstone National Park. The products of the American packing towns would fill a train reaching from New York to Spokane.

The automobiles and trucks moving by freight would fill one solid transcontinental train and a second one reaching to Pittsburgh, while the wheat so moving would fill one transcontinental track and another one reaching half way across the continent.

Iron ore would demand 4,300 miles of cars, while coal and coke would require a train 40,000 miles long.

The variety of the requirements of the American people is no less remarkable than the volume of those requirements. On the list of commodities hauled by the railroads there are more than 8,000 different items, which embrace every kind of product, from abas, worn by Arabs as garments, to zymoscopes, used by zymologists as ferment-testers.

WHERE THE GEOGRAPHIC COMES FROM

Under the blessings of adequate transportation the interchange of products is amazing. For instance, take so simple a thing as your copy of the NATIONAL GEOGRAPHIC MAGAZINE.

The paper is made in Massachusetts, from pulp-wood grown in Canada, treated with acids coming from half a dozen States, and coated with clays coming from England and Florida.

It is printed with presses made of steel wrought in Pennsylvania, from pig iron extracted in Ohio, with the aid of limestone from Michigan and coal from West Virginia from ore mined in Minnesota.

The glue for the rollers of the presses comes from the trimmings of skins brought from India, China, and South America, including goatskins, beef hides, and horse hides. The glue for pasting on the cover comes from Pennsylvania, where it is manufactured from raw materials coming from as widely separated points as Cape Town, South Africa, Aden, Arabia, and Buenos Aires, Argentina.

The ink is a lesson in geography all by itself. It is made of carbon gas black from Louisiana; linseed oil from Minnesota, Argentina, and India; mineral oils from many American oil fields; vegetable oils other than linseed, from the cotton belt and China; dryers from Brazil and Canada; dyes from various States; and gums from New Zealand, the Dutch East Indies, and the South.

The type metal is made of lead from Missouri, copper from Montana, tin from the Straits Settlement, and antimony from Japan.

WHY MOST OF OUR FREIGHT MOVES EASTWARD

Handling freight trains is an interesting task from the layman's standpoint, a hard one from the trainman's point of view, and an involved one from the yardmaster's aspect of the work.

With a tremendous export balance and such a large percentage of the country's population massed along the eastern seaboard, it is inevitable that much more freight has to move eastward than is dispatched westward. How to keep the car supply adjusted without unnecessary westward movement of empties is one problem, and how to prevent empties from moving eastward after they have discharged westbound loads is another.

In a recent year the freight trains of the countiy ran, in round numbers, 51,000,000 hours. Each train ran about 72 miles a day at 10.5 miles an hour, including stops and waits.

The making up and breaking up of the vast number of trains that move each 24 hours are constantly being accelerated through the installation of improved freight yards.

Formerly, all tracks in these yards were level, and a train was broken up or made up, as the case might be, only by innumerable switch-

A FREIGHT YARD IN THE ANTHRACITE REGION: CARBONDALE, PENNSYLVANIA

Coal, coal, coal, and more coal! One carload of freight out of every four that the railroads haul is coal to supply America's demands for heat and power. It is an interesting fact that there is a close agreement between the number of train miles, the number of tons of freight, and the number of passengers hauled by the railroads of the United States. In 1920 the Class I railroads, which embrace all but a few minor short lines, moved their trains 1,237,000,000 miles, hauled 1,255,000,000 tons of freight, and carried 1,234,000,000 passengers.

ings back and forth. In the new "hump" yards much of this is done away with. A train comes in off the line. It is backed up to the top of a steep grade. Here, mayhap, a score of tracks spread out from the one on which the train stands, each connected with it by a series of switches, or a "ladder," as these switch series are known in railway parlance.

Then one by one or group by group the cars in the train are uncoupled and allowed to roll by gravity down the ladder and onto the several tracks on which all cars of common destinations beyond are being gathered. These

tracks are known as classification tracks. To one go the cars bound through to Chicago; to another those with St. Louis as their destination; to still another those having transcontinental destinations. And so it goes (see illustration, page 95).

GETTING FREIGHT OVER THE ROAD
IS NOT CHILD'S PLAY

Whether the cars being sent by gravity down the incline and onto their respective tracks are from a train that has just rolled in or from scores of sources, each goes to its particular

RESULT OF A REAR-END COLLISION AT SULPHUR SPRINGS, MISSOURI

Automatic train-control devices that mechanically stop trains on the safe side of the danger line when the engineer fails to do so are in daily operation, with such positive results that the Interstate Commerce Commission is taking steps to make their installation compulsory on all the main railroads. These controls warn against defects in the tracks, causing broken circuits, as well as against defects in their own apparatus. Furthermore, they exclude all trains from any block occupied by another train. The Chicago & Eastern Illinois has had a whole division equipped for several years, with a record of not a single collision on the tracks thus protected.

track, and one switching crew with one engine does the work that six crews and engines do in the old-fashioned yards.

And it is well that things can be speeded up, for in 20 years the freight business of the American railways has increased threefold and is still expanding.

In one yard not long ago 121 eastbound trains, with more than 3,200 cars, and 78 westbound, with 3,600 cars, arrived in 24 hours—a train every 7½ minutes; and of course these had to be broken up and made over into about as many other trains.

To the train crew the caboose is a "hack," and most crews have their "pet hacks." When the end of the division is reached they usually get a load back, but if there is nothing in sight the engine runs light" back to the other end, sometimes taking the caboose along.

Getting freight over the road is hard work at best. Ask the firemen who have to fire the engines through the Baltimore tunnels of the Pennsylvania how often one of their number shows up unconscious after a trip through these gas-filled bores. Ask the brakeman who has to toil through the night with rain and cold as companions as he walks the long platform atop his train.

But at worst, think of 40 transcontinental trains snow-bound and idle in the single State of Wyoming! Think of 25 feet of snow on the level and 50 in canyons and gulches! Think of thermometers in which the mercury tries to hide itself from the frost, in weather where zero temperature would seem moderate by contrast!

Yet through it all the engineer must have an unobstructed vision; the fireman must shovel an unwonted quantity of coal into the firebox; the brakeman must protect his train, operate his

switches, and always be ready if the air-brakes should fail to work. Water tanks become masses of ice without and freezing water within.

On one line 40 miles of telegraph poles were broken down by a snow and sleet storm, most of them falling across the tracks. On another every bridge and trestle for miles was carried down stream by an unrelenting downpour.

Snow time is worst of all. When the weather forecaster sees a big snow storm in the offing he acts as intelligence officer for the railroads, and they begin to marshal their forces for the fray. Every engine in every roundhouse must have steam up, ready at an instant's notice to take the road and help to keep the rails clear. An ounce of prevention was never worth a fuller pound of cure than in fighting the snow. The division superintendent becomes a general, and mobilizes the last ounce of his reserves in motive power and men.

Trains are shortened, and the intervals between them cut down. If the flakes come too fast for such strategy in keeping the line open, the engines are equipped with ordinary plows, which buck the drifts and push them to one side.

But if the hordes of the snowflake armies become so numerous as to overwhelm even these, the big rotary plows are sent into the fray. These possess great cutting wheels able to drill a bore whose diameter will permit the passing of a train.

Shoved forward by perhaps three engines, a rotary plow eats its way into a big drift, discharging the snow through a giant nozzle that extends out over the right of way, and throwing a stream of flakes that would engulf an ordinary building in short order. Therefore it is built so that the nozzle-man can regulate the di-

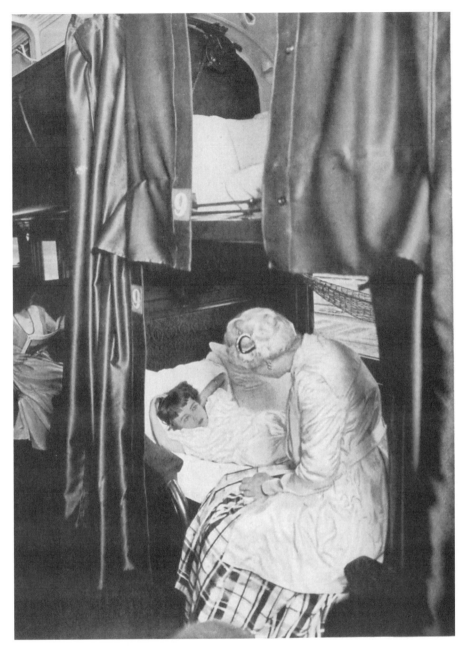

A BERTH IN A REGULATION PULLMAN

The average passenger on the railroads of the country makes the equivalent of five round trips between Baltimore and Washington annually. The trains that carry him run faster, but are slower earners of money than the freight trains that must give him the right of way. The passenger trains earn $2.78 for every mile they run, against $6.81 earned by the freight trains.

rection of his stream and thus avoid such catastrophes.

In the terminals and freight yards a snowstorm means frozen frogs and out-of-commission switches. Brooms, oxyacetyline blow-pipes, and such have to be called into service, and a stiff battle must be waged if trains are to be kept moving.

Latterly, experiments have been made in the direction of installing electric heaters at switches, and one of the foremost terminal superintendents in the country tells me that he be-

lieves the day is not distant when snow will be deprived of its terrors, so far as terminals are concerned.

A VAST ARMY OF TRAVELERS

The story of the passenger traffic of the United States is one of a volume of business no less astonishing in proportions than the freight traffic.

Imagine the vast array of folk who ride over the rails of the country in a year transformed into an army of marching troops, in solid for-

BUILDING THE EMBANKMENT APPROACH TO THE BURLINGTON'S BRIDGE
ACROSS THE OHIO RIVER AT PADUCAH, KENTUCKY

The modern methods of making the high fills that save heavy grades are as much in advance of the old mule-and-scraper method as the Burlington's Southeastern Express is ahead of the first train the C., B. & Q. ever sent across the Missouri River.

WAR WORKERS IN THE RAILROAD YARDS IN JERSEY CITY

In 1916 the average railroad worker labored 3,151 hours and received $854.20. In 1920 he worked 2,630 hours and was paid $1,820. The railway army in 1920 was more than two million strong. One hundred men working every minute from the dawn of history to the present hour would not have put in as many hours as did the railroad employees in 1920.

mation and 257 abreast. The rear guard of that vast army would be waving their farewell to the skyline of New York as the advance guard was hailing the Golden Gate at San Francisco, if the line of march were an air line. Truly, 1,175,000,000 passengers is an imposing multitude of people!

And the aggregate miles they traveled! In its annual marathon around the sun, the earth is about the speediest thing we know. It hurtles through space at so great a gait that it covers a distance equal to that which stretches between Ottawa, Canada, and Tallahassee, Florida, in a single minute. And yet, even with such a speed record, it cannot pile up mileage as fast as the American people in their railroad travel.

Indeed, if the earth were to speed up its gait eighty-fold its annual mileage would be no more than equal to the 46 billion miles covered by the travelers of the United States in a normal year.

There are many things about passenger traffic that constitute wonder stories of the transportation industry, concerning which lack of space forbids even a mention. The tales of the time-table, the baggage business, the ticket-sellers, the sleeping-car service, to say nothing of scores of other activities, must go untold.

But there is one phase of passenger travel that arrests the attention of everybody—that of the modern passenger station in a major city.

To visit one of these big terminals and there to study the art of handling vast throngs of humanity and amazing numbers of trains, to go down into the dispatcher's office, out to the information bureau, and through the whole plant, indeed is an experience not to be forgotten.

South Station, in Boston, with its 45,000,-000 passengers and 196,000 trains a year, holds

the American record for volume of traffic. North Station, in the same city, with its 32,000,000 passengers annually and 400 trains daily, holds the record for a station serving only one road. Union Station, in St. Louis, with 22 roads entering it, holds the record for the number of lines served.

But in their modernity, in the intricacy of the problems solved, in their construction and operation, in the probable future expansion of their patronage, no other stations in the world claim as much interest from the public generally as the Pennsylvania and Grand Central stations, in New York.

The Pennsylvania is the largest terminal under one roof in the world; but the Grand Central, with its two levels, covers double the acreage of the Pennsylvania. The latter was built as a railroad station pure and simple, while the former was constructed as a real-estate development, which should provide every possible convenience known in the art of transportation, and to surround the station with associated interests, such as hotels and office buildings.

The New York Tunnel Extension of the Pennsylvania, with the station and its appurtenances, cost about $115,000,000, while the Grand Central cost $75,000,000. By the broad idea of making a business center on the land redeemed by electrification, and that which had to be condemned to provide for the underground trackage, the Grand Central Station, with its group of surrounding edifices, has been made a self-supporting institution.

THE STORY
OF GRAND CENTRAL STATION

A trip through the Grand Central Station is a revelation. Every day 600 trains arrive and

RADIO ON THE RAILS

Some of the progressive railroads are installing radio receiving stations on their big through expresses. It is now even proposed to put in a motion-picture service in dining-cars, so that when those who answer the last call of the "white coat" have finished their meals the car may be converted into a motion-picture theater for the benefit of those who have wearied of the car-window panorama and of the books and magazines they brought along to relieve the tedium of the trip.

depart; 33,000,000 passengers pass its portals in a single year. Its public rooms have an area of six acres and its main concourse could accommodate 15 regiments of infantry. Its facilities are so arranged that no passenger need retrace a step—ticket window, Pullman office, checking-room, all coming in their order on the traveler's way to his train.

While, of course, the primary purpose of the New York Central was to build a great

station, with an ultimate capacity of upward of 75,000,000 passengers a year, yet electrification made it possible to reclaim 40 acres of land in the very heart of upper Manhattan—all over the two levels of the 32 miles of terminal tracks—and to utilize this area for the biggest single civic development in the history of architecture.

The main station building, whose suburban and express levels are connected by long in-

A HOLIDAY CROWD IN THE GRAND CENTRAL STATION, NEW YORK

Only once in history have the doors of the new Grand Central Station been closed. That time a storm too heavy for even the greatest of railway organizations to conquer stopped traffic, and the string of commuters, waiting for a way to get home, was strung for miles down the avenues leading to the station. The station authorities figured that the people were safer in the snow outside than in a possible panic inside.

clines, or ramps, instead of by stairs, has a veritable labyrinth of inside streets and passages lined with shops and stores. One can, without going out of doors, reach three subways, three hotels with 3,000 rooms, a series of office buildings housing 6,000 workers, and two big university clubs.

Great as has been the development of the reclaimed areas by the construction of office buildings, hotels, clubs, stores, and apartment houses over the station and approach tracks, vast additional structures are expected to rise. Even the main concourse itself was built with a view

of ultimately surmounting it with a 17-story office building.

One of the remarkable things about the construction of the Grand Central is that it was built as a substitution. The whole structure and its satellite buildings had to go up, their predecessors had to be torn down, and the substitution of electricity in the place of steam had to be wrought while passengers were coming and going and trains arriving and departing.

Vast yardages of stone and dirt were blasted and moved, amazing tonnages of structural steel and hollow tile and brick were removed

A MODERN INTERLOCKING SIGNAL TOWER

The interlocking signal system has contributed no mean share to the reduction of the time of trains between terminals. If they had to thread the modern maze of tracks in the average city, with every switch hand-thrown and every signal hand-set, accidents and delays without number would occur.

here and put into buildings there, but traffic went on as though nothing could happen.

There are hundreds of superlatives about the Grand Central Station to which space does not permit even a passing reference.

But surpassing everything else is its work of handling 600 trains that come in and go out every day. To get a faithful picture of that task, one must take a few notes to begin with.

The two-story railroad—for that is what it amounts to—in the terminal is entirely below the street level. The second story tracks are 34

feet below the street level and the lower story tracks 55 feet.

On the upper level there are 41 tracks and on the lower 22. In addition to these, there are 62 other tracks on the two levels used for storing engines and cars, with a big loop on the lower level, built so as to permit trains to be turned around without shifting or backing out of the station.

Under the old way of railroading, men had to set switches and signals by hand, out on the track itself. Then came the tower, with its le-

THE MEN WHO CONTROL A MODERN CLASSIFICATION YARD

This push-button machine controls the maze of switches and tracks of the clearing yard near Chicago (see illustration, page 95).

vers enabling a man to set them at a distance, but still by hand.

But manifestly, with 238 different sets of points and crossings, 570 signals, and 1,200 train movements, on 113 tracks, every railroad day, the very latest equipment had to be installed—indeed, had to be invented to meet the situation.

And the human element had to be eliminated. One slip of the hand, one lapse of the mind, and a wreck would be almost inevitable. So mechanisms had to be devised that would make it impossible for signals and switches to conflict. Plans had to be worked out that would make it impossible for one train to get into a block occupied by another.

The result was the development of what is probably the most complete switch and signal layout in the world. Men send trains in and out of the station without seeing them.

Some distance out of the station the four tracks over which trains come to Manhattan Island spread out into ten tracks, four of them leading to the suburban level, 55 feet below the street, in the station, and the other six to the through-train level. Here an interlocking tower controls the ten tracks. Three-quarters of a mile nearer the station, the four lower-level tracks spread out into 22 and the six upper into 41.

Here, under 49th Street, is located the largest interlocking plant in the world. The machine controlling the suburban-level tracks has 400 levers. That on the floor above has 376.

The director of these tracks has a long case before him, covered with frosted glass, on which is outlined the entire track and switch layout of the territory under his command. It is drawn to scale, and little lights at their appropriate positions tell the director the condition of each track, whether occupied or vacant.

Whenever a train passes over a switch, its lights go out and do not shine again until the wheels have passed over the next switch ahead and have extinguished its lights in their turn.

There are many levermen whose duty it is to manipulate the 400 levers that operate the switches and signals, as the director calls out the tracks he wants the trains to take.

These men see neither the tracks nor the trains on them, and possess no picture of the track transformation their operations result in. To put the average train onto its appropriate track in the station requires the manipulation of twenty-odd levers, each in its own particular order in the sequence, while some of the more complex berthings may take sixty-odd lever movements.

But so deft does practice make these men's brains that they never hesitate. They manipulate the levers as precisely as a professional pianist touches the keys of his instrument.

But even if the lever man were to try to move any lever of the combination out of its proper order, he could get no response from it, for it is so locked that it cannot be moved out of its sequence or wrongly.

Imagine a piano whose keys could be so interlocked that each note of each piece had to be played in its proper order!

The electric lights on the frosted glass chart are interlocked and arranged in such a way that the trains passing over switches automatically duplicate the track situation for the director.

FOLLOWING A TRAIN
INTO THE STATION

Let us watch a train coming into Grand Central Station from New Haven.

When it passes Mott Haven Junction the director of the big interlocking station at 49th

THE OLD HAND-BRAKE METHOD OF CONTROLLING A TRAIN

Nothing has added more to the success of railroading than the air-brake. Some time ago a demonstration with a train of 100 cars, each of 120 tons capacity, was made. It was shown that air-brakes on even such a train could stop it more quickly and more smoothly than a man at every brake-wheel of the train could have done.

Street gets a message telling him what kind of a train it is, how many cars, etc., and the time it passed the junction.

When the train reaches 72d Street it automatically closes a circuit that turns on an electric light in the director's cabin at 49th Street, advising him that it is ready to be a "guest in his house." He thereupon looks at his frosted glass diagram, determines what track is available, and calls out his orders to the levermen.

As soon as this is determined the fact is written on a telautograph, which duplicates the information to the bulletin-board and other points around the station, advising the 200 or more porters, baggage-men, and others on what track and at what minute the train will stop.

Among loud-speaking telephones, telegraph instruments, and electric lights, the interlocking station director is a commanding general who is in constant touch with every sector held by his forces.

All the switches and signals must be set positively before the leverman at the "piano-box," as the mechanism is known, can lock the switches.

At the Grand Central Station trains leave on schedule time. No wait is made for belated passengers. The gates close and the train goes, each at a predetermined time. A red light near 45th Street signals the closing of the gates.

Train dispatching at the Pennsylvania Station differs somewhat from that at the Grand Central. Here the tower spans the tracks and the tower director sees the trains he guides in and out of the station.

It is a fascinating experience, though one conducive to high stepping, to be privileged to go down through the maze of tracks and third rails to the big tower, where the trains are guided into and out of the big station.

Here one may see the whole track layout, from the New Jersey portal of the Hudson tunnels into the station. Instead of a frosted glass diagram, as at the Grand Central Station, one finds the tracks themselves in miniature. Every switch is in its appropriate place and every signal also; and as the leverman throws the switches on the steel highway itself, the ones on the brass miniature move in harmony. Every part is built, and every motion is made, to scale.

As one stands in the big tower a signal light goes out as a big limited leaves the Hackensack Meadows and begins its plunge under the Hudson. The director of the Jersey tower reports its passage and the station-tower director gives orders to the levermen, who set the switches for the track on which the train will roll into the station.

With watch in hand one observes the course of the train through the Hudson tube. As it starts into the tube the speed increases, as is shown by the rapidity with which the miniature signal lights go out and come on again, for the tubes swing down deep under the Hudson.

Then, as the lowest point beneath the river is passed and the train begins to climb the steep grade up to the east bank, it slows down rapidly. Light after light goes out, stays out until another ahead of it is darkened, and then shines again, proclaiming the fact that the block ahead of it is clear.

Presently in rolls the big limited, right under the big tower, and several hundred people flock out of it, little thinking of the wonderful mechanism that stands guard over the maze of tracks and switches and never fails to send each train into its appropriate berth.

With regret one leaves untouched a hundred and one phases of railroad operation that would add to the picture of the vastness of the

CASTLE GATE, ONE OF THE PICTURESQUE PASSES IN THE ROCKIES

The work of the men upon whom devolves the task of locating a railroad across the Rockies is dramatic in the extreme. Here they must be lowered into deep and forbidding canyons to plot the steel way; there they must climb precipitous slopes into the snow fields, to run their line; but all the time they must keep in mind the fact that when their work is done luxurious passenger trains and heavy freights are some day to pass there on curves so gentle that the soup of the fastidious folk in the diner may not be spilled, and over grades so easy that long strings of freight cars can be moved with a reasonable amount of motive power.

THE CHIEF ENGINEER AT THE THROTTLE

President and Mrs. Harding have done less traveling than most of their immediate predecessors in the White House. When the railroads were turned back to their owners the Government released to them property that cost more than twice as much as the Allied debts to America, and which probably could not be replaced for twice their original cost.

task of moving the nation's freight and carrying its passengers, as well as of the intricacy of the details of a year's transportation business. But the phases that have been considered are representative as well of those which must be passed by. The economics of railroad operation are beyond the scope of this article.

RAILROAD DEVELOPMENT IN AMERICA

The history of railroad transportation in the United States is a story of amazing development. At the outbreak of the Civil War the country had less than 31,000 miles of line, of which only about 2,000 were west of the Mississippi. It was not until February 22, 1863, that the first sod was turned in the projection of the first transcontinental line, on the Pacific end at Sacramento; and not until December 2 of the same year that work began in the Mississippi Valley.

Six years later, after many vicissitudes and after 225 miles of overlapping line had been built, an agreement was reached whereby the two companies joined forces, and the golden spike which tied together the East and West was driven at Promontory, Utah (west of Corinne), on May 10, 1869.

The railroads, indeed, constitute the key that unlocked the treasure-house of American resources. The story of the nation's rise to greatness and power is an account of a succession of frontiers.

At the beginning the frontier stopped at the Blue Ridge Mountains. The turnpike and the canal finally pierced these heights and let it move on to the Alleghenies. These became an isolating influence that held the pioneers in the eastern half of the Mississippi Valley almost a separate people from those on the Atlantic seaboard until the railroad builders' faith removed these mountains, as far as the flow of commerce and communication was concerned.

In turn the Mississippi River became the frontier. What was the good of the land west of the Father of Waters if that stream remained unbridged?

Even as late as the early eighties our people thought that it was useless to build railroads through western Minnesota and the Dakotas, arguing that the region was a desert in summer and a wilderness of snow in winter; and it took Custer's campaign against the Indians to persuade the public that the Northern Pacific extension beyond the Mississippi, at St. Paul, could be kept open more than five months a year.

During the Civil War the South had much less than a third of the nation's railways. Furthermore, these linked up distant communities rather than industrial centers. Comparatively few of them were strategic, whereas the North had rail connections admirably fitted both for the movement of men and munitions and for the interchange of commodities essential to the fabrication of these munitions.

In Europe the history of railway construction has been that of roads laid down to meet the demands of traffic already there. In this country tens of thousands of miles of line have been built through virgin territory, which it was hoped would grow up to their facilities.

Linking the ore of the Minnesota mines and the coal of the Pennsylvania mountains, the farms of the Mississippi Valley with the markets of the Atlantic Slope, the trucking and fruit-growing districts of Florida and California with the consuming centers of the East and the North, the geography of railway traffic in America has been developed along lines that eliminate distance and make the whole United States one great homogeneous community, tied together by bands of common interest, as are the people of no other equal area in the world.

Far-flung as are the boundaries of the United States it is now possible to interchange commodities between any two places within those boundaries with less transportation costs than were paid between relatively close communities a hundred years ago.

The United States has about one-sixteenth of the earth's land and an equal proportion of its population, yet it has nearly a third of the world's railway mileage. Its population is only one-fourth that of Europe, yet it has almost enough miles of line to duplicate the systems of Europe and Asia together.

FURTHER READING

William E. Leuchtenburg, *The Perils of Prosperity, 1914–1932* (1958) traces the events which transformed America from an agrarian to an industrial nation. See also Peter Lafferty and David Jeffries, *Top Gear: The History of Automobiles* (1990) and Ray Spangenburg and D.K. Moser, *The Story of America's Railroads* (1991).

INDEX

CONTRIBUTORS

General Editor FRED L. ISRAEL is an award-winning historian. He received the Scribe's Award from the American Bar Association for his work on the Chelsea House series *The Justices of the United States Supreme Court*. A specialist in American history, he was general editor for Chelsea's *1897 Sears Roebuck Catalog*. Dr. Israel has also worked in association with Arthur M. Schlesinger, jr. on many projects, including *The History of the U.S. Presidential Elections* and *The History of U.S. Political Parties*. He is senior consulting editor on the Chelsea House series *Looking into the Past: People, Places, and Customs*, which examines past traditions, customs, and cultures of various nations.

Senior Consulting Editor ARTHUR M. SCHLESINGER, JR. is the pre-eminent American historian of our time. He won the Pulitzer Prize for his book *The Age of Jackson* (1945), and again for *A Thousand Days* (1965). This chronicle of the Kennedy Administration also won a National Book Award. He has written many other books, including a multi-volume series, *The Age of Roosevelt*. Professor Schlesinger is the Albert Schweitzer Professor of the Humanities at the City University of New York, and has been involved in several other Chelsea House projects, including the *American Statesmen* series of biographies on the most prominent figures of early American history.